500

Tips
for
Getting Published:
a guide for educators, researchers and professionals

500 Tips from Kogan Page

500 Computing Tips for Teachers, [...] Race and Steve McDowell
500 Tips for Further and Continuing Education Lecturers, David Anderson, Sally Brown and Phil Race
500 Tips for Getting Published: a guide for educators, researchers and professionals, Dolores Black, Sally Brown, Abby Day and Phil Race
500 Tips for Primary Teachers, Emma Packard, Nick Packard and Sally Brown
500 Tips for Quality Enhancement in Universities and Colleges, Sally Brown, Phil Race and Brenda Smith
500 Tips for Research Students, Sally Brown, Liz McDowell and Phil Race
500 Tips for School Improvement, Helen Horne and Sally Brown
500 Tips for Teachers, Sally Brown, Carolyn Earlam and Phil Race
500 Tips for Trainers, Phil Race and Brenda Smith
500 Tips for Tutors, Phil Race and Sally Brown
500 Tips on Assessment, Sally Brown, Phil Race and Brenda Smith

500

Tips

for

Getting Published:

a guide for educators,

researchers and professionals

DOLORES BLACK, SALLY BROWN, ABBY DAY AND PHIL RACE

KOGAN PAGE

London • Sterling (USA)

First published in 1998

Kogan Page Limited
120 Pentonville Road
London N1 9JN
and
22883 Quicksilver Drive
Sterling, VA 20166, USA

British Library Cataloguing in Publication Data

A CIP record for this book is available from the British Library.

ISBN 0 7494 2637 3

Typeset by Jo Brereton, Primary Focus, Haslington, Cheshire
Printed and bound in the UK, Biddles Ltd, Guildford and King's Lynn

Contents

Acknowledgements   vii
Introduction   1

Chapter 1   Getting started with your writing   4
1   Why do you want to publish?   6
2   Some reasons for getting published   8
3   Getting and using the right equipment   10
4   Deciding what to write   12
5   Collecting your source material   15
6   Ordering and structuring material   18
7   Planning time to write   20
8   Preparing to get started   22
9   Tackling the blank page   25
10   Maintaining momentum   27

Chapter 2   Writing choices   29
11   Why write collaboratively?   31
12   How to write collaboratively   33
13   Monographs   35
14   The delights of popular publishing   37
15   Conference proceedings   40
16   Journals   42
17   Edited collections   44
18   Selecting papers for publication   47
19   Communication matters   49

Chapter 3   Writing books   51
20   Targeting a publishing company   53
21   Getting an overview   56
22   Using information sources effectively   58
23   Guidelines on proposal contents   60
24   Writing a good proposal   63
25   Book proposal timescales   65
26   Thinking about the international dimension   67
27   Establishing a market for your book   69
28   Marketing your book   71
29   Working with your publisher   73
30   Publication dates and launches   75
31   Book contracts   77
32   Money matters   80

Chapter 4   Writing for journals   **84**
33   Targeting the right journal   86
34   Making your research publishable   88
35   Using the literature search effectively   90
36   Finding the right voice   92
37   Style points   94
38   Improving your 'hit rate'   96
39   Responding to referees' feedback   98
40   Dealing with rejections   100

Chapter 5   Getting it right   **103**
41   Introductions, forewords and prefaces   105
42   Getting the language right   107
43   Getting feedback on drafts   110
44   Manuscript appeal   112
45   Diagrams, drawings and tables   114
46   Making a good finish   116
47   Getting the references right   118
48   Writing a glossary   120
49   Compiling an index   122
50   Checking proofs   125
51   Copyright and rights   128
52   What *is* publication?   131

Chapter 6   Electronic publishing   **133**
53   New models of publishing   134
54   Advantages and disadvantages of electronic publishing   136
55   Publishing in e-journals   138
56   Using electronic means to support traditional publishing   140

Conclusions   **143**
And the last word...   **145**
Further reading   **147**
Index   **149**

Acknowledgements

The authors are grateful to many participants in their workshops on 'Getting Yourself Published' in the UK, Australia and New Zealand, for many useful suggestions and ideas, and to Gordon Wills for sponsoring writers' workshops. We are particularly grateful to D Royce Sadler for a great deal of wise feedback, Maxine Alterio for some off-the-wall ideas, and to Neil Fleming for valuable suggestions. Our thanks go to Vina Mayor for telling us that we had missed out advice on 'Deciding what to write' in our pilot edition, and to some workshop participants at Crown Agents who presented one of us with this problem which led us to write some solutions! We are also grateful to Mary Prior and Mark Saunders for their useful feedback and encouragement.

Introduction

There is no sensation in the world like the first time you see your name in print. Even well established authors get a thrill from receiving a letter of acceptance from a journal editor, or ripping open a parcel containing the first copy of their latest book, or discovering someone they don't know reading something that they have written. Almost everyone believes they can write for publication, yet most people don't do it, and this book is all about helping you move from being unpublished to breaking into print.

However, only *you* can do it (unless you are sufficiently rich or vain to afford ghost writers). There is nothing magic in the process. Getting published is – as the old cliché goes – 90 per cent perspiration and 10 per cent inspiration. We offer you here more than 600 tips on making the breakthrough.

Each of us writes and enjoys writing. We hope to share with you our enthusiasm. We are each individual writers, and we hope also to share this with you. This means that, although we agree on most things to do with writing, we have our different ways too. Therefore in this book we have written down the differences as well as the similarities to give you a richer menu of options to choose from. When you see an apparent contradiction between things we have written in different parts of this book this is deliberate, and we hope it will help you all the more to find your own preferred approach to getting yourself published.

Who is this book for?

We have kept in mind a wide range of prospective authors during our work on this book, and their differing kinds of need for information about publishing. The people we hope to help include:

- academics wanting to make a start on getting their names known in their respective specialist fields of study, or under pressure to get their work published to raise their level of security in institutions where funding is linked strongly to publishing output;

- professional people in any area writing in their technical or specialist subject area, for example, accountants, careers advisers, business and management consultants, public relations, marketing experts, and so on;

- people with a specific technical or vocational skill who want to write a book on it either for a general interest audience or for a specialist one. Such people may be as different as expert chess players, landscape gardeners, arts and

1

crafts practitioners, cooks, interior designers and so on, all sharing the need to find out about how to get their writing under way successfully.

In short, our book addresses the situations of most authors of specialist, academic or general-interest non-fiction works. Many ideas in this book will be equally relevant to authors of fiction, especially those parts about the creative processes of writing, but with the exceptions that fiction publishers normally require complete manuscripts for consideration, and fiction writers usually work through agents in their dealings with publishers.

What does this book cover?

Our first chapter provides advice on the very earliest stages in the process, clarifying in your own mind what is your rationale for wanting to get published, so that you can target your efforts appropriately. It then leads into the pragmatics of making a start. Not least in this chapter we have included some tips on how to work out what to write about, in case you haven't already got some definite ideas.

In the second chapter, we provide a range of choices about how you write (collaboratively or alone), the nature of the medium in which you plan to publish, from the joys of popular publishing, through conferencing proceedings and journals, to edited collections. We also provide insights on how choices are made about selecting material for publication, and how best to communicate with other stakeholders in the process.

Chapter 3 is all about writing books, from first ideas to the launch of your book, with plenty of advice about how to get your ideas for a book accepted, and about the financial aspects of publishing, which new authors often overlook.

Our fourth chapter concentrates on the area that many academics focus on most intently: getting published in journals of the right status, to make a difference to their professional lives and progression.

In Chapter 5 we get down to the nitty gritty of actually producing a manuscript, including here all the elements that often get forgotten in the excitement of writing a book, but which frequently make the difference between a mediocre and an excellent publication.

Finally in Chapter 6 we look to the future of publishing as electronic formats become more prevalent. This short chapter discusses the pros and cons of using the Internet alongside or instead of conventional paper-based formats.

This book isn't really designed to be read from cover to cover. We expect readers to pick it up and start at the point at which they are currently most log-jammed. Do you want to write, but can't decide where to start? Are you finding it difficult to tackle the blank page? Are you confused about how to target the right journal? Is it better to write alone or collaboratively? Dip in and out of these tips as they most appeal to you, and then let the advice prompt you to move back to your own writing that you may well have been putting on the back burner as your read this as a work-avoidance strategy! Use the book as scaffolding to help provide a supportive framework for your writing, and then remove it, so that your work stands alone once it is complete. Then you can enjoy the process of getting yourself published.

Chapter 1   Getting started with your writing

1   Why do you want to publish?
2   Some reasons for getting published
3   Getting and using the right equipment
4   Deciding what to write
5   Collecting your source material
6   Ordering and structuring material
7   Planning time to write
8   Preparing to get started
9   Tackling the blank page
10   Maintaining momentum

There are thousands of reasons put forward for *not* having got published, many of which boil down to reasons people give for not having managed to actually get started on their writing. Most of these reasons are actually excuses! In this chapter, we wish to disarm you regarding many of these excuses. More importantly, we hope to help you to find some good reasons why you should get down to and get started with your writing, and then to arm you with some techniques for helping to make it a more straightforward process for you.

Our first two sets of suggestions are about *why* you may want to get yourself published. It is important to have some good reasons – ones that will see you through the harder or more boring parts of the overall process. We offer a number of reasons for you to select from, but you will probably already have a clear idea of your own aims, too. We follow this discussion with some suggestions about equipment. Things to do with this are often quoted as reasons (excuses) for not getting started writing, but for some writers having the tools they want are an effective incentive.

What are you going to write about? Most successful writers have just too many ideas, and always have something that they hope to write when they have time after writing what they are currently doing. Many writers (including ourselves) always seem to be working on several different writing projects at once, and this is useful as when we get bored or frustrated writing one thing there's always something else to tackle for a change. The boring thing may take that bit longer as a result of this, but other things get done. We wrote this book quite quickly, partly because we enjoyed doing it so much that we let some less inspiring things slip! However, there are people who want to write, or need to write, who just don't know what to start on. We can't tell them what, but we have some suggestions which will help them work it out.

Next, we look at ways of getting your source material together. Our set of suggestions on this is just a starting point; we will return to collecting and organising information in several parts of this book. Having collected your sources together, we look briefly at ways of ordering and structuring your material. This, too, is something that will be a recurring theme in this book, and in the present chapter we are just trying to help you to make sure that you start as you mean to go on.

The most frequent reason (excuse?) that people give us for not having got themselves published is that they have not got the time it takes. People are indeed much busier nowadays than used to be the case in many walks of life. The secret is to manage time, and to make the most of reasonably small elements of time, when it is not possible to sit down undisturbed for lengthier periods.

Our next set of tips is on 'Preparing to get started'. We hope that these suggestions will prove useful to even the busiest of people; they are based on practices that busy authors find productive. Nothing will happen until the first blank sheet of paper has something written onto it (or until there's a first-draft file in the computer's memory). 'Tackling the blank page' offers a variety of ways of making sure that your writing really does get started.

We end this chapter with 'Maintaining momentum' – some suggestions to help you to keep going once you have started.

After exploring and trying out those suggestions from this chapter that you find most relevant to your situation, and most in keeping with your personality, you can dip selectively into other parts of this book, depending on whether you are writing for journal publication, putting together a book, or trying your hand at other kinds of writing. You may, however, wish to find out more about how writing works in practice by exploring Chapter 2: 'Writing choices' first. But will this be a work delaying strategy? Only you will really know!

1

Why do you want to publish?

Love, fame, fortune... what is it that will drive you to put hours, weeks, months or even years of time and energy into your publishing effort? Knowing this can help you remain motivated, and will also help you shape your work for the right purpose and audience. Most authors find it hard to articulate just what their reasons are, but maybe the following ideas will prompt you, especially if you're an academic doing research. If not, more ideas follow in our next section.

1 **Take time to allow yourself to dream up as many motives as possible.** There is no right or wrong motive, only the one that appeals to you the most. Set yourself a few hours to spend alone testing your motive against some of those below – or even some we haven't thought of ourselves.

2 **Is it a driving ambition to be widely-recognized for your research?** Nothing wrong with that – ego and the desire for recognition drives most human beings much of the time. If this is your prime motive, you may have to set yourself a long-term goal. Publishing is a slow process, but can eventually bring acclaim and notoriety, and lead to more work for you if you are a self-employed consultant of any kind.

3 **You believe that you really have something new to say?** Or perhaps you've finally taken the hint from your department head or supervisor? That's fine, too. These are the very people paid to promote the careers of other academics besides themselves. But, having appreciated the not-so-subtle nudge towards action, don't neglect Tip 1 above. You'll need strong personal reasons to embark on this process.

4 **To publish or to perish?** A good publishing record enhances your value as a researcher and academic. It demonstrates two important attributes of your role: your ability to conduct worthwhile research, and your ability to focus your effort sufficiently to turn that research into a published paper.

5   **Your institution's recognition increases with the number of its staff who publish.** Your published works, therefore, benefit your university or research centre and, in turn, that benefits you. It fuels the funds for further research and the likelihood of increased international collaboration amongst academics worldwide.

6   **Trying to publish for the first time invites rejection.** That's an excellent reason to do it. Rejection by a good journal is usually accompanied by clear guidance about why your paper wasn't suitable, and often includes direction about how to do it better next time. Where else can you receive such eminent free advice?

7   **Offers to present conference papers usually go to those who are already published.** Just getting yourself on the conference circuit will not only enhance your reputation but will bring you into contact with peers interested in your work. Many lifelong professional associations are formed at these events.

8   **People may actually read what you have written.** Understandably, you may feel that the published paper is the end of the process, but more often it is only a beginning. People interested in your work will sometimes contact you just to offer feedback, make a suggestion or ask a question.

9   **You may even read what you've written.** Most prolific authors say that the writing process is helpful primarily to force their own thinking and clarity of expression. The very act of summarizing and explaining your work makes it clearer in your own mind.

10   **Self-confidence.** You wouldn't be reading this book unless you had a need to publish – for any or more than the above reasons. Having done it, you'll feel that you have fulfilled an ambition. And that feeling will make the next paper that much easier.

2

Some reasons for getting published

'Why do I want to get myself published?' is a sensible question for readers of this book to be asking themselves, and we started to address this question in our previous set of tips. To help you to analyse further your own motives and driving forces, we've replied to some of the *answers* that people give to this question. Maybe we've covered one or more of your own motives below?

1   **'To make money.'** We've put this reason first, because it's the impression that people get, especially when thinking about writing books, but it's actually far from the truth! The royalties cheques authors usually receive for most non-fiction works might only pay for a week's groceries once a year. So if this was your reason for getting published, abandon it now, unless you know that you're destined to be the next guru in your field!

2   **'To get my work known.'** This is a good reason. That said, there has to be an audience out there wanting or needing to find out about your work. It is true however that publishing books, articles or scholarly papers are the ways that your work can make its mark.

3   **'Because I want to get a better job.'** This follows on from wanting to get one's work known sometimes. Being published and recognized in a particular field can be a passport to job opportunities in fields where shortlisting and interviewing criteria rate published scholarship highly.

4   **'Because I have something to say.'** This is one of the strongest reasons. When authors wish to share a passion with others, and when they wish to change the state of the universe in their particular corner, there is not much that will block their way to successful publication. Nevertheless, it is still important to evaluate whether anyone wants to listen.

5   **'Because I've been told to.'** This is quite a common reason nowadays. Lecturers in universities and colleges, for example, are under considerable pressure to publish, so that their institution scores well in evaluations of research productivity. The imperative to publish is often passed down to individual members of staff, and 'publish or perish' is a phrase that is heard only too often.

6   **'Because I like writing.'** This is a good reason for trying to get published. There is no denying that there is a sense of satisfaction when one's writing appears in print. Many writers find the process quite addictive, and get to feel quite uneasy at any time when they've not got something or other in the process of being written.

7   **'Because I think I can do it.'** For many authors, publication starts quite late in their lives, and is often prompted by having read others' works for some time, and gradually gaining the feeling that 'I'm sure I can do at least as well as some of this!' It's never too late to start on the pathway towards publication.

8   **'Because I've done a lot of the basic hard work already.'** Many people have already accumulated material that is just waiting to be distilled into published work. Most of the real work has often been done already, and the business of turning it into a publishable form is more an administrative process than one of creation.

9   **'Because I love to travel!'** This is not as unlikely a reason as it might appear. One of the happiest benefits of being published is that authors are invited to talk about their work in distant places (rather than close to home, for some reason). The rewards of travelling and meeting new people who are interested in your work may far outweigh such mundane matters as royalties.

10   **'Because I want to be famous.'** This is a perfectly valid reason for writing and getting published. Many people *have* become famous this way, and there is absolutely no reason to prevent this happening to you. Of course, people sometimes become *infamous* instead, but it's probably a risk worth taking!

3

Getting and using the right equipment

All you actually *need* to get going with some writing is paper and pen or pencil. That said, most writers nowadays use keyboards of one sort or another. The following suggestions may help you to decide what you really want for your writing, or perhaps convince you that you've already got everything you actually need.

1   **Don't wait till you've got your ideal equipment.** For some potential writers, putting off the moment of starting to write is achieved by using lack of equipment as a work avoidance strategy.

2   **Go for a computer rather than a typewriter.** Even if your old typewriter (manual, electric or electronic) works well, the time you will save by being able to edit on-screen rather than re-typing makes it more or less essential to have a computer. Also, it is useful to be able to print out as many copies as you want of a document. If you can already type, learning to use a word-processing package is relatively easy. Don't be put off by the weight of the manual; most writers learn best just by having a go (and making mistakes).

3   **Ask around.** It's well worth asking other authors about which word-processing package they use and why. Don't forget, however, that most people will want to convince you that the one they use is the best (they don't really want to tell you that they may have made a wrong choice themselves!).

4   **Check what your publisher thinks.** Publishers are accustomed to receiving work from authors on computer disk, even though they still usually expect paper-based versions for copy-editing as well. Ask what word-processing packages your publisher is used to handling. It's well

worth avoiding the problems associated with having to find someone to translate your writing into another format before your publisher can accept it.

5   **If you are co-authoring, check what packages your co-authors are using.** While it is possible to translate from almost anything to anything else, such procedures get in the way of editing each other's work, or adding in sections to something written by a co-author.

6   **Think about what you really need.** Most modern word-processing software has far more power than is actually used by the vast majority of writers. If you are planning to use a laptop computer, all of this extra power may reduce drastically the effective battery time available to you.

7   **Get something you like the feel of.** Whether you're buying a laptop or a desk computer, you may spend many hours using the keyboard. It is worthwhile making sure that you are going to be comfortable as you write; this will also help to keep you at it.

8   **Remember that your new equipment will very soon be dated.** Computers and software go out of date very quickly, mainly because manufacturers and retailers want everyone to keep buying new products. Therefore, think twice before paying extra money for the latest technology, and only do so if you are quite sure that you actually need it.

9   **Decide what printer you will need.** If you have ready access to such equipment at work, you may not need to purchase your own. However, most writers like to see how their material looks as soon as possible after writing something, and it is worth looking at the sort of printer which will be easy to maintain, not too bulky, and which will be able to print everything you normally need.

10 **Only choose a colour printer if you need to print colour.** This may seem obvious, but unless you're sometimes going to print coloured overheads, for example, you're probably better off with a black and white model.

11 **Ink-jet printers are cheaper, lighter and quicker than laser printers.** Not many people notice any significant difference in print quality. It's also far easier to change ink cartridges than some toner cartridges.

4

Deciding what to write

We almost forgot to write this section! Once your momentum as a writer is going, this just isn't a problem. The problem becomes deciding what to get on with writing and what to leave on the back burner. Here are some suggestions that we have found helpful to some people who wanted to write or needed to write, but had no idea what topic to start writing about.

1   **Don't make 'not knowing what to write' become your writing avoidance strategy.** Thousands of people have already done this, but they aren't too well known as a result of this! We know many people who are perfectly capable of writing, and who have a lot to tell the world, but who have never got down to choosing a topic to write about *and* actually making a start on it as suggested below. Left to themselves, they will probably never start – at least until someone confronts them with their work avoidance strategy. Have we confronted *you*?

2   **Have something to help you not to forget your ideas.** Once the ideas start flowing, they can occur to you at any time and in any place. Have some way of getting them down on paper, where you won't lose them. A small notebook that will fit into a pocket, briefcase or handbag is useful. Loose bits of paper too easily get lost or mis-filed, but are better than nothing if an idea strikes when you haven't got your book with you. Menus have been used by great writers and composers! Whenever an idea occurs to you, jot it down in your book. The important thing is to write even a couple of words down about each idea you have, to avoid the frustration of 'knowing that I had something interesting but now it's completely gone from my mind'.

3   **Brainstorm a range of draft working titles.** Review your reasons for wanting to get published, and for each of these jot down a few draft working titles which could become the start of some writing. Don't worry at this stage about whether you feel able actually to write on these titles. Build up a collection of things you may some day *want* to write, or *need* to write, or simply *be in a position* to write. Don't ever feel that there is

anything you won't some day be able to write about if you want to. Add to your list anything you're writing already, such as a project proposal or a report, which may turn out later to be a good start towards something publishable for a wider audience.

4   **Think creatively.** All of your draft working titles don't have to be sensible! In fact, it's often the rather way-out ideas that turn out to be most interesting to write up, and there's more chance that you may have something original if it's rather unusual. Include topic ideas that you know quite a lot about, but also topics that you may simply want to find out about.

5   **Do an importance rating for each of your ideas.** It is worth doing this regularly from time to time. For example, rate each idea on a scale 'H', 'M' and 'L' for 'high, medium and low' against a range of factors, such as importance in the context of your job, importance to your boss or manager, fun, relevance to solving a problem or need, having something you really want to share, being already well set up with relevant data or information, and so on. You could then award an 'H' three points, an 'M' two points, and an 'L' one point, and work out which of your draft ideas has the highest score at that moment in time. This may be a reason for starting with that idea, or equally a reason for exercising your right to start with exactly which idea you feel like starting with!

6   **Shortlist no more than half-a-dozen possibilities.** You can still go back and re-visit other ideas on your back-up list. With each of your shortlisted ideas, write the draft working title in an oval in the middle of a blank page in your little notebook. Maybe then add a few further ideas about how to make the titles more interesting or punchy. You don't have to choose the actual title for a long time yet.

7   **Start fleshing out your working titles with ideas.** Draw spokes radiating from the titles, and add at the end of each spoke questions, keywords, and other very brief reminders of your thoughts (no more than a few words to remind you of each thought). These questions could be the things you would need to research as a basis for your writing. The keywords could remind you of things you already know which you could include in your writing.

8   **Regard all of your fleshing out as changeable.** You don't have to stick with any of your original ideas about detail when better or more interesting ones come along. You can change the questions that your writing will address when more important ones occur to you, or when you find that you don't want to, or can't, address some of your first thoughts.

9   **Review your identified possibilities.** They will, by now, give you quite a lot of help regarding where to make a start. The draft working title with most detail may well be the best place to start writing. On the other hand, sometimes you will have found that for some working titles you now know enough about it to make an informed decision that you *don't* really want to get started on it, or at least not yet. Don't throw away any ideas, their time may come later, even years later.

10   **Start getting feedback on your draft ideas.** Talk to anyone you can who may be able to help you find out more about your own working titles, and about things you haven't yet thought of about them. Get a friend or colleague to interview you about your ideas. Jot down questions that they ask you that would be worth including the answers to in your writing. Jot down any of their ideas that you may want to use. Keep a careful note of whose ideas you may use, so that you can acknowledge them in your final writing.

5

Collecting your source material

Some people seem to manage to collect source material all of their lives, yet never get round to getting their material published. Since you are now reading this book, you are not likely to be one of these people. We hope that the following suggestions will include things of value to you in your own quest to get your act together ready for the process of getting your work published.

1   **Polish your information retrieval skills.** Using online library catalogues, consulting the catalogues of publishers with a strong list in your subject, and checking recent issues of key journals all help to ensure that you minimize the chance of missing a key publication that you need to refer to. You can do a lot of similar research by making effective use of the World Wide Web.

2   **Work outwards from the centre of the web.** It's usually productive to work out who are the key authors in the field in which you are going to publish, and see whose work they most commonly cite. This is often more efficient than just relying on database keyword searches.

3   **Make good use of citation indexes.** These allow you to start from a key paper or source, and to work forwards in time to find articles that have cited it. The chances are that these more recent papers will also be relevant to your search.

4   **Aim for a 'read once' approach for each item of material.** Try to make a decision whether or not you're going to collect or discard an item, rather than put it aside to consider again later. You can have a 'perhaps' file for those pieces that really do need further consideration, but your aim should be to avoid wasting time over rereading the same things.

5   **Keep good records of who wrote what.** Card indexes or computerised databases of relevant books, papers and articles are invaluable to an author. It saves a great deal of time when you can get the exact bibliographic details you need to be able to refer to any of your sources. Collect these details in the format that is used in journals that you may intend to publish in yourself, so that when you are making a list of references your task is made easy.

6   **Annotate your list of source materials.** It's easy to forget just who said exactly what about what! As you read others' writing, make your own notes of particularly important ideas that you may wish to refer to in your own work. It can be particularly useful to select phrases or sentences you may wish to use as direct (acknowledged, of course) quotations.

7   **Be meticulous in your attributions.** All important ideas and arguments that are not your own must be acknowledged and referenced.

8   **Make your own 'importance ratings'.** Work out your own code along the lines **** for a source which is really relevant, authoritative and important, down to * for a source which may deserve a passing mention.

9   **Don't throw anything useful away.** The key word here is 'useful', of course. In turn, this means that you need to have an idea about what you may want to publish, so that you can start to collect and store relevant nuggets. Don't, however, just accumulate heaps of potential material. It is really important to be focused and systematic about your data right from the outset.

10 **Start to organize your collection of source materials.** It can be useful to collect together materials in labelled folders or wallets, so that you have all the bits and pieces that you'll need for writing a particular chapter or section in one place. Writing a short list of the contents on the front of the folder, and keeping it up to date, can save time when you're looking for exactly where you've stored a particular source.

11 **Work within the copyright laws.** Be especially careful not to exceed 'fair use' limitations on the amount of material that you can quote from another source without permission. It is almost invariably the author's responsibility to obtain such permission, but your publisher may have ideas on how you should ask for this when necessary.

12 **Criticize carefully.** If you need to comment negatively on another's work, do it sensitively. Avoid anything that could be interpreted as libellous, or that could give rise to a possible lawsuit.

13   **It's never too early to write draft paragraphs.** When working through your source materials, whenever you have an idea of the gist of something you may want to write yourself about the source or its content, sketch out your key thoughts in a sentence or two, which may be turned later into a paragraph somewhere in your own writing.

14   **Don't plan to start at the beginning!** Starting-off your masterpiece is a crucial task, but one which is best done when you know what you have actually written! It's best to stitch together ideas in the middle of your proposed writing, and gradually work both backwards to where you will begin and forwards to your endings.

6

Ordering and structuring material

There's an old saying people quote about making presentations: 'tell 'em what you're going to say, tell 'em, tell 'em what you told 'em'. Written work follows the same format, with a beginning, a middle and an end. Here are some suggestions which we hope will help you to plan what goes at the beginning, in the middle and at the end.

1   **Wrap it all up into 20 words or less.** Before plotting the detail of your structure, make sure you are clear about the purpose of your work. You may assume you know this, but unless you can write it in a clear, simple, statement, you do not yet have the clarity so essential to guide you.

2   **Begin with what interests the reader.** Pieces which begin with your name or the name of your college or company are not reader oriented. For example, it won't interest the reader to hear that 'Company X is completing research on a new drug to help people with migraine headaches' as much as it will to read 'People who suffer with migraine headaches may soon be helped by a new drug being researched by Company X'.

3   **Tell them where they're going.** The introduction is designed to let your reader know your purpose, why it's important and to whom, and what they will gain by reading your material. For longer articles or books, the introduction should contain an overview of how the material is structured.

4   **Establish credibility.** Before developing the main body of the work, tell the reader why it has any validity. If it's a research paper, who did it? If you're quoting other sources, who are they and why should anyone care?

5   **Create your case.** As you approach the main argument, theory, proposal or findings, tell the readers how or why you, or your sources, arrived at it. Readers need to be reassured that the methods used were sufficiently robust or generally acceptable to support the case being presented.

6   **Summarize regularly.** At frequent intervals, tell the reader where you've got to. This will reinforce the points you are making and help readers maintain concentration. A confused reader who needs to ask 'what on earth are they saying now?' is not going to appreciate your work, or even finish reading it.

7   **Follow AIDA.** A tool used by many professional authors reminds us of this simple order: A for Attention (get the readers); I for Interest (pique the readers), D for Desire (make the reader want to know more); A for Action (tell them what they can do about it).

8   **Don't neglect the implications.** Following the main body of your book or paper, you must do more than summarize what you've told your readers. You need to spell out exactly what it means to them, answering the 'so what?' question that lurks in their minds. So, how will all this affect a scientist/manager/teacher/researcher? And what can they do about it?

9   **Always check for the six key questions.** Who, what, where, when, why and, sometimes, how. If your work covers these questions, you've probably said just about everything that is important. Work out what is the best order in which to cover these questions in the context of your own writing.

10 **When in doubt, leave it out.** Writing with economy means you must be prepared to edit your work and have it edited for you. Ensure that your salient points are just those, and you don't bore or confuse your reader with tangential or supplementary information. It's really worth having that 20-word summary that we mentioned at the beginning of this set of suggestions to help you to decide what to leave out.

7

Planning time to write

You can write an excellent article or chapter in a day or two. Whether it's 1000 or 7000 words doesn't matter, except that shorter pieces usually take longer. It's just that much harder to express in a few words what you could easily write about endlessly. Given that, why is it we so often say we don't have time to write? Is it time we don't have, or energy, or focus, or confidence? Here are some suggestions about how to get started.

1   **Decide to do it.** Successful people usually say that when they are committed to a project the work proceeds with little effort. Being half-interested or even grudgingly accepting of the task will ensure that it takes more time and more energy, and that the finished product will be less than satisfactory. Agree with yourself that you will do it, and reinforce your commitment by telling others.

2   **Decide on your focus.** If you don't know what you want to say, it will take more time to say it and the result will be vague, if not garbled. Consider and revise your focus until you can blurt it out in a single statement of purpose without hesitation.

3   **Plan your work.** Pay particular attention to all the tips in various parts of this book concerning planning articles, papers and books. Create an outline which follows the logical process discussed in 'Ordering and Structuring Material'. A few notes for each heading will do.

4   **Remember how many things, in real life, get done in the last 10 per cent of the available time.** This means that they may only actually take 10 per cent of the time that you thought they would take. It also means that it's possible to get most things done in the *first* 10 per cent of the available time, and have all the rest of that time to get on with other things!

5   **Think in terms of small blocks at a time.** The thought of sitting down to write 10,000 words would faze any writer. But sitting down to write 200 words? That's easier.

6   **Open your daily planner.** Look through your schedule and tick off blocks of time, of no more than two hours. Even one hour will allow you to write a significant amount if you have followed the above steps. Half an hour is a good way to start.

7   **Commit to the schedule.** Your writing blocks are as important as any other commitment. Even if you choose short blocks of 30 to 60 minutes, you will be further ahead than you were before.

8   **Unplug the phone, close the door...** Remove other distractions for your brief, but intense, writing sessions. It's too easy to be interrupted, and then the interruption becomes an excuse not to continue. Everyone can live without you for an hour or so.

9   **Try not to exceed your allotted time.** Inspired as you may feel, a tired writer is a poor writer. It is far better to stop when you had planned to, rather than continue until the effort becomes greater and the session grinds to a halt.

10   **Plan to edit later.** Switching from writer to editor is difficult. It can also become a source of discouragement. Your well-trained critical mind will dismiss quickly any awkward sentences and half-formed arguments. That will be useful later on, but can cool your enthusiasm and self-confidence at the earlier stages.

11   **Schedule time for peer review.** Any piece of writing, from a newspaper article to a monograph, is greatly improved after the writer gains feedback from others. Make sure you allow time to share your work with others and incorporate their suggestions.

12   **Plan time to celebrate!** Mark the end of your writing project with a well-deserved party. Treat yourself and your supporters. Congratulate yourself and thank your family, friends and colleagues who respected your time. You'll need them again!

8

Preparing to get started

Writers often feel it is difficult to break through the 'blank page' syndrome, finding it tough actually to make a start. Here are some ideas to get you going. Don't work through them in the order we've written them in; each of them is meant to be a different way of hyping yourself up for starting, or actually getting started. Try out those which appeal to you most, then use the ones that work best for you.

1   **Use a piece of wallpaper.** Stretch it pattern side down on the floor, and lay out your notes, resources, texts you will refer to and other material along its length, at positions indicating approximately where in your writing you will use them. This way you can get a good overall picture of what you are writing. Once you have moved things around, and more or less decided on the order, write onto the wallpaper what will appear there, and then cut the wallpaper up into manageable lengths.

2   **Start early.** Systematically collect the sources you may refer to by using a card file or software package to keep them in order. Having easy access to the details of your sources helps to make the task of starting to write much less daunting.

3   **Begin by reviewing what is already written.** This may well be the basis for your review chapter, and is often worth making into a paper or article in its own right.

4   **Don't feel that you need to start from the beginning.** Once you have a shape for your writing, start where you feel most comfortable. Move backwards and forwards among the various areas around your starting point, writing drafts of what you want to say.

5   **Try making writing a daily habit.** It then does not matter if some days are much more productive than others. Your day's contribution does not have to be done sitting at a computer or in your favourite writing location.

Ideas scribbled on bits of paper in the most unlikely surroundings can still be edited into your writing, and the ideas may be just as good as those that come to you when you're 'seriously' writing.

6 **Don't spellcheck while the creative juices are flowing!** Spell-checking quells the fires of creativity, and is best done when you've got nothing better to do.

7 **Don't expect to get a first draft straight away.** Give yourself the freedom to write a very rough draft first, which you know to be imperfect, and which you will edit much further later. It is easier to remedy obvious errors and deficiencies in your own work than to start from a blank sheet.

8 **Make a list of 'damn fool' questions you might want to answer.** These might include 'What is the background of this research?', 'What evidence is there to support this theory?', 'What did I do?', 'How well did it work?', 'Who else has done work in the area?', 'What are the implications of their work for mine?', and so on. Start writing your answers to these questions, then delete the questions replacing them with headings such as 'Background', 'Research Data', 'Evaluation', and so on. You will then have a really rough draft that can be revised and expanded.

9 **Get someone to interview you about your work.** Make notes of their questions and your answers. It may help to use an audio recorder to help you to remember the main points. Use the most important questions and answers to help you to form a draft agenda for your writing.

10 **Read all about it.** Do some background reading and keep careful records on a card index or data book. Use Post-it notes stuck into your texts or articles to mark sections you may wish to quote, and to jot down comments you will wish to make, and areas you need to cover. Then use these as a basis for the part of your writing which reviews the literature.

11 **Make a scrapbook folder.** Collect together photocopies, cuttings, images, graphs, data and text that provide a background for what you are writing about. In the first instance, don't worry about trying to put the materials into any logical order. Then set aside some time to browse through your scrapbook, and let this help you to draft a plan for action.

12 **Make some lists.** Before you start trying to write connected prose, you might find it liberating to start with lists of pros and cons, historical data and current research, likely authors you might want to quote, key areas you might like to cover, and so on. Use these lists as triggers for your writing.

13   **Lay an egg.** This is a powerful mind-mapping technique, and helps you to keep to the point in your writing. We've already mentioned the value of this in 'Tip 4: Deciding what to write', but let us remind you in case you did not see this because you'd already made your decision. On a blank sheet of paper laid sideways (landscape) write the key question or issue about which you are going to write in an oval at the centre of the page. Then draw lines radiating out from the 'egg' and jot keywords or phrases at the end of these lines to outline the principal sub-areas that relate to the central issue. Elaborate on the keywords as necessary. Once you have a busy page, try to order the elements in a way that makes sense to you, and then start to write them up.

14   **Brainstorm your ideas onto a flipchart.** Either on your own, or with a co-author, or a tolerant friend, jot down ideas in a fairly random order onto a flipchart, aiming for volume of ideas at this stage. Don't go for any censorship; include daft and impractical ideas too. Pick up and elaborate on ideas that arise, and let your mind(s) range free. You can next try to map on to your flipcharted brainstorm a logical structure that you can use to translate your ideas into connected ideas.

9

Tackling the blank page

Writers are often pictured at their desks in a state of feverish activity, sweat dripping from the brow, seized by inspiration and guided by an almost supernatural energy. Yes, writers have flashes of inspiration, just as do teachers, bank managers and checkout operators. But most of the time they do their work professionally and with discipline. Here are some suggestions about how to handle that moment when the blank page or grey screen taunts you.

1   **Remember, there's no such thing as writer's block.** There is only planner's block. No one, not even the most practised writer, can feel comfortable looking at a blank page if he or she doesn't know what to say. Our tips on 'Preparing to get started' should make sure you have something definite in mind for that blank page.

2   **Writing is not an out-of-body experience.** No one will get those words onto paper except you. There is no muse sitting on your shoulder whispering your lines. Accept that it is your professionalism which will get the job done, not an other world gift of inspiration or creativity.

3   **Review your plan.** Before you begin to write, you need to have a clear sense of what you want to say and how you will say it. Those thoughts should all be noted against your outline or overview. Refresh your memory.

4   **Don't start writing until you know what you want to say right then.** You will be disappointed and frustrated if you think that at any moment you can simply switch on your computer or pick up your notepad and watch the writing flow. Choose one part of your plans, and get going just on that bit, at least to start with.

5   **Create an objective for each session.** Before turning on the computer decide which section you are going to write. You should have already planned the time available, so decide now how you are going to use it best.

6   **Expand your notes for your selected section.** Before starting to write, detail key points that you want to cover and the order in which you intend to cover them. Don't worry about getting every word right, but make sure you have your ideas sorted out.

7   **Take one line at a time.** Even if you have created a well-structured outline, the task of writing for an hour might still seem onerous. The journey of a thousand words starts with a single sentence. Allow yourself to gain a sense of achievement; however much you write in a single session, it is still progress.

8   **Take one page at a time.** Try to concentrate only on the specific section you are writing in the time you have allotted yourself. It's confusing to race ahead to further chapters or sections when you haven't finished the few paragraphs which face you.

9   **Make notes for further sections, but don't write them in full.** As you try to concentrate on the page in hand, jot down notes on a separate piece of paper if they come to you and leave them for later. It's easier to get the ideas off your mind and onto a different page to review later.

10 **Remind yourself why they invented wordprocessors.** Part of the supposed 'writer's block' is the anxiety we feel about not getting it right. Don't worry about it. Whatever you write first is only your first draft. No one will see it but you. What have you got to lose?

10

Maintaining momentum

Tired writers create tired readers. Learning how to pace yourself and your work will help you to create and maintain momentum. These tips address both the writer's personal momentum and the momentum of the piece.

1   **Remember, focus brings energy.** Cluttered thoughts are enervating. As you try to make sense of the mess in your head, you burn up energy through effort and the inevitable frustration you create. If you actually get as far as writing down the clutter, you will confuse and tire your readers.

2   **Start with attention.** Work on your single purpose sentence until it is lively and vivid. Starting with something which will grab your readers' attention will make them sit up and take notice and eagerly move on to the next paragraph to find out more.

3   **Remind yourself of your purpose before each session.** To maintain your own energy and momentum, refresh yourself with the single statement which describes so perfectly what you are saying and why it's important. (If you've not done this yet, refer to earlier tips.)

4   **Tell your readers why it's important.** You may be so convinced of your purpose and argument that you take it for granted. Keep your readers' interest by spelling out the implications or impact of your subject.

5   **Keep quiet.** Now that you've actually started to write, resist the urge to talk about your article or book. The more you talk about it, the more you dissipate your excitement. You will also find that the act of orally communicating the idea or story makes the written task less exciting.

6   **Take your readers on a journey of discovery.** Everyone loves a story. Let your story unfold little by little so that your readers have a clear understanding of what's happening at any given point, and a sense that there's something even more interesting to come.

7   **Imagine the questions readers ask.** Momentum is easily lost when readers have to stop and question something you've just said. You may have introduced a piece of jargon, for example, or a concept that is foreign to your readership. Pretend your reader is there with you asking obvious questions. Answer those questions in sequence.

8   **Pause for refreshment.** Just as writers need to manage their time carefully to sustain their energy, so do readers. Make sure that you ease back after introducing a major concept, and reinforce it before moving to the next idea. This will help your readers to absorb it and retain concentration.

9   **Vary your rhythms.** Follow long sentences with short ones; short paragraphs with long ones. Varying the flow will help your readers maintain focus – and it will help you, too. Once you adopt a single style for too long, it becomes stale and tedious.

10   **Forget about it.** Once you've finished a writing session, turn off the computer and leave the work. Try to absorb yourself in other activities and don't talk or think about your writing project. It's more important to approach each session feeling refreshed than to let it take over your life.

Chapter 2   Writing choices

11   Why write collaboratively?
12   How to write collaboratively
13   Monographs
14   The delights of popular publishing
15   Conference proceedings
16   Journals
17   Edited collections
18   Selecting papers for publication
19   Communication matters

In this chapter, we aim to help you to explore some of the many possibilities open to you as a writer. We start our chapter with two sets of suggestions about 'Collaborative writing', showing first some reasons for working with other authors rather than by yourself, then some ways of going about it. We, ourselves,very much enjoy writing collaboratively, and that is how this book came about. We also believe that our writing is much better as a result of our collaboration than if any one of us had tried to write the book by ourselves.

We continue this chapter with some suggestions on writing by yourself. 'Writing monographs' can be somewhat lonely, and can require considerably more persistence, perseverance and determination than when you have other people who will keep you to task. However, there are perfectly valid reasons for writing on one's own, and we've all done it ourselves, too.

Our next section is on 'The delights of popular publishing'. Such writing may not impress fellow professionals in one's field, but it can be great fun. It can also get your work to a much wider target audience than an erudite paper in a scholarly journal.

Many authors first start writing in the context of putting together the background to a conference presentation they may be giving for inclusion in published conference proceedings. This can be very good practice for writing for scholarly journals, and we hope that our suggestions will make the task less daunting. We then move straight on to the important matter of publishing in journals. Many readers of this book may be under considerable pressure to publish in this way, and research funding (and indeed continuing employment) may well depend on success in this area.

Our next set of suggestions relates to making contributions to 'Edited collections', which has many similarities to writing for journals, but with the additional need to write so as to fit in to the overall shape and style of the collection.

Our last two sets of suggestions in this chapter look at things from the other side of the fence. In 'Selecting papers for publication' and 'Communication matters' we offer suggestions to *editors* about how they may go about working with authors and reviewers. It may be the case that this book will be seen by few experienced editors, but we hope that the sort of advice that we would offer them will be of even more value to you as an author, helping you to see a little more of how editors' minds work.

11

Why write collaboratively?

There are advantages and disadvantages to writing collaboratively, some of which we share below. As authors who frequently write this way, it is only to be expected that we think it is a good idea, but then we would, wouldn't we! Here are some pros and cons to help you make your own minds up.

1   **You can cover more ground.** You can share out the workload, with co-authors working to their own areas of strength. Two (or more) heads are often better than one, and your joint areas of expertise are likely to be broader and stronger collectively than individually. You can also share out the drudgery like the compiling of the index and the checking of proofs.

2   **You keep each other on target.** It's quite easy to backslide when the only person who will suffer is yourself, but it's harder to let down a co-author. One of the delights of co-authoring is that you help to keep each other going when motivation is flagging and the armchair or the beach (or marking) beckon urgently.

3   **You can edit each other's work.** Giving each other feedback at intervals throughout the process is enormously developmental. You can copy edit each other's work, as it is easier often to spot gaps and difficulties in someone else's work than it is in your own.

4   **It can be a lot of fun.** People who write collaboratively do well to choose co-authors with whom they can get on well socially. This means that a writing weekend can include a lot of laughs as well as a great deal of serious graft. Even those who do most of the work at a distance on paper or electronically often find there's a lot of pleasure in working with like-minded people.

5   **You get to know people better.** Working closely with co-authors over the extended period of time that it takes to write a book can develop acquaintanceships and cement friendships.

6   **The pace at which the book is written can be speeded up.** Two or more people working simultaneously can produce work at a prodigious rate without loss of quality, especially if they are editing each other's work.

However...

7   **You need to choose your co-authors carefully.** Some are unscrupulous, lazy and ineffectual. It is a good idea to have a very clear plan before you start regarding who will do what, so that the parameters are quite clear in advance. This usually saves problems later.

8   **Squabbles can break out over minor details.** People can have very strong feelings about minutiae, for example whether to use US or Anglicized spellings of words or whether parenthetical dashes are acceptable – and these can cause conflicts disproportionate to the supposed crime!

9   **Order of authors on the cover can cause difficulties.** Co-writers have been known to argue, often at the very last stage about whose name should go first on the cover. This can be very important in terms of individual's research outputs. You really need to sort this out well before you start. Just using alphabetical order always privileges the early alphabet surnames. Publishers may also have a view on this, often wanting the most established author as first named in order to boost potential sales.

10   **Those who review research outputs often have a dim view of co-authoring.** Under some national systems, co-authored work counts for much less than monographs, despite the fact, as we would argue, that co-authoring often results in better work. In the UK system, for example, it matters a lot whether your co-authors come from the same institution as you in terms of evaluations of research productivity.

12

How to write collaboratively

If you decide to write collaboratively the process needs to be effectively managed if it is to work well. These tips are designed to help you to do this.

1   **Play with the ideas first.** When you are making your first cautious stabs at a book proposal or the outline for an article, rough out your ideas on paper together, brainstorm the content on a piece of flipchart paper or allow yourselves a long rambling conversation. Allow yourselves to free range in the early stages.

2   **Map out the territory.** Once your ideas have started to come together, think about how the different elements fit together. Many authors find it easiest to do this visually on a whiteboard, or on a large piece of paper or on A4 sheets spread all over a table. This will help you move things around so that you can achieve a logical order.

3   **Don't commit yourselves to a rigid framework too early.** It's very easy to get bogged down in what seemed like a good structure in the first place, only to find it unwieldy once you start to write. Try to build in some flexibility so that you can change the shape to some extent once you have started the process.

4   **Decide to what extent your work is to be collaborative.** Publishers usually prefer texts that have a unity of style, rather than two or more voices in the book. If you are writing completely separately, you will need to work out how to provide linking material to bring the book or article together as a cohesive whole.

5   **Gain agreement early on pragmatics.** Make sure you agree on what kind of referencing system you are using, whether references will be at the end of each chapter or collected at the end of the book, whether you will include footnotes, and what kinds of illustrations or diagrams you will include (if any).

6   **Ensure you are compatible electronically.** It will save hours of work if you are able to swap disks with ease, read each other's work sent electronically and send each other attachments to e-mails. If this is not possible, you will have to set up communications systems that work for you and mean you don't waste time struggling to make incompatible formats agree.

7   **Edit each other's early drafts.** Try to make sure you see and comment on sections of each other's writing fairly early in the collaborative process. This will help you get a feel for each other's writing and prepare you to make adjustments of style if you are writing in very different styles.

8   **Learn to give each other positive strokes.** One of the delights of writing together is that you can encourage each other with positive feedback and congratulate each other on progress so far.

9   **Learn to give each other robust feedback.** This is also essential in order to assure the quality of the writing. It is often difficult to challenge something your co-author has written, but it is much worse to live with the consequences of having your name attached to something with which you are unhappy.

10   **Use project management strategies to keep the writing on course.** It's not a bad idea to have a wallchart to map progress, or at least to have checkpoints in your diary at which you can actually or virtually discuss progress to date, how to cope with unforeseen difficulties and how to modify the original shape of the writing to incorporate new research or changing circumstances.

11   **Be prepared to bale out if it isn't working.** There are some collaborations that are destined to fail and it's a mistake to continue with them once things have broken down irretrievably. Try to get out of the situation with as much dignity as you can, retrieve what you can to use elsewhere (after discussing it with your former co-author) and learn from the experience so you can choose a more compatible co-author next time.

12   **Plan to celebrate your success when the book or article is completed.** You don't need to go to the extent of an elaborate book launch, but it's important to mark the completion of the process in a celebratory way. This may also provide the occasion to plan for your next collaborative project.

13

Monographs

Writing a book on your own is a choice many authors make, taking into account the points in the earlier section on 'Why write collaboratively'. The rewards are great, leading often to high prestige, recognition by your peers and sometimes even substantial royalties. However, in order to write a monograph, you will need to have or develop the following:

1   **Something worth saying.** Any book of whatever length needs to have at its heart something that is really worth communicating, if it is to have any readers. It isn't enough for you to feel you have something to say in your work, you have to assure yourself (and your publisher, and your readers) that it is worth hearing.

2   **A powerful desire to do it.** Unless you really want to write a book, it will be difficult for you to complete it. Many people, and most academics, have at least one half-written book stashed away that they started, but just didn't sufficiently want (or need) to complete, so it was shelved for the time being.

3   **Strong self-motivation skills.** You need to be able to plan and organize your work in such a way that you can structure your writing systematically. Unlike writing a PhD, when a supervisor keeps a watching brief on your work, you will need to be your own progress chaser and your own tough task orientater.

4   **Helicopter vision.** It is important to be able to take an overview of what you are writing, standing back from time to time to ensure that you can clearly see how all the disparate parts of your book fit together. It is very easy to get so close to what is being written currently that other parts of the book seem difficult to relate to and distant.

5   **Tolerance from those around you.** Writing a book can make you self-centred, single-minded and difficult to live with, especially when deadlines loom. To write a monograph, it helps a lot if you have the support of partners, family and work colleagues.

6   **Stamina.** Writing a book alone takes high energy levels and 'stickability'. It can be a lonely process, which can also be very hard on the hands, the back and the psyche.

7   **Feedback from others.** In most cases, it is a great mistake to present any manuscript to a publisher which has been seen by no eyes other than the author's. It's usually useful to test drive elements of your book with helpful peers who can help you to recognize the errors and omissions that are often difficult for authors themselves to see.

8   **The ability to make time to do the task.** Every writer will find a hundred competing tasks that will get in the way of writing. Authors who succeed in getting a monograph published are those who make time in busy lives to undertake all the stages of writing that are necessary to get ideas into print.

9   **Finishing skills.** Once the manuscript is written, that is only the tip of the iceberg as Chapter 5 of this book suggests. An author working alone needs to recognize that preparing an index, checking proofs, clearing copyright elements and finalizing references represent an enormous amount of work, just at the time when you want to rest on your laurels after all the hard work of writing.

10   **A thick skin.** Writing a monograph means that there is only one person to take the criticism that will inevitably be levelled against your book. However, the upside of this is the fact that all the glory of a well received book will also fall on your shoulders.

14

The delights of popular publishing

The discipline of writing for general interest popular magazines and journals can be both challenging and rewarding for any author wanting to write on a specialist topic for a wide audience. There are suitable outlets for every aspect of most subject fields. The style of writing required will be very different from that, for example, for an academic journal. You may need to practise a more active, lively and personal approach in your writing.

1   **Don't regard popular publishing as unworthy.** Many a professional or academic has sniffed at the so-called 'popular press' as something beneath the stature of an esteemed scholar. Nothing could be further from the truth. Many esteemed scholars write for publications aimed at general audiences, and find both the discipline of doing so and the rewards worthwhile.

2   **Look for the angle.** How would you describe the benefits or implication of your ideas, theories or research to someone without any background in your speciality? Practise on your family and friends who are not connected to your field. If they can't grasp the fascination of your work in a single sentence, chances are no one else will either. It's just this attention to focus and impact that will make your article fresh and interesting.

3   **Who wants to know?** Popular publications are read by busy people, people like us. We are usually reading for entertainment or to satisfy our need to appear informed and up to date. Try to picture potential readers: what do your ideas or theories say to a teacher? To a manager? To a minister?

4   **Go to the library to discover the wide range of popular publishing.** Magazines exist not only for general audiences, but sub-sets of those audiences – not just people interested in boating, but people interested in wooden boats, and, of these people, those who are interested in meteorology… can you see your research on weather patterns in the north Atlantic having a whole new meaning for the yachting community?

5   **Read the writers' handbooks.** These digests, available at most bookstores, contain annually updated information on everything from weekly news magazines to poetry quarterlies. You will find helpful summaries of each publication telling you precisely what they are looking for, who to contact and how much (if anything) they pay.

6   **Create a query letter.** The above manuals will tell you how to do this. You will create a short synopsis of your proposed article, describing its purpose, content, audience and treatment. The aim is to attract the editor's attention by showing how well you understand and can satisfy the readers' needs.

7   **Resist the urge to mass mail.** Anyone who sends out a press release or a synopsis to more than one publication simultaneously has missed the point. Your article needs to be directed at a specific audience to be meaningful. Besides, most popular publications are competitive and don't want to publish the same article as another publication in their market.

8   **Buy wallpaper paste.** Most successful writers say that they could have papered their walls with rejection slips before they received an acceptance. By targeting the popular press you have entered the most crowded market possible. Editors receive hundreds of unsolicited queries and manuscripts every week – some, every day.

9   **Comply with the editor's advice.** When you do, on the first or fiftieth occasion, receive a positive response, stay humble. Now is not the time to second-guess the advice your editor gives you. No one knows the magazine or newspaper better than he or she. If you are asked to trim your proposed 1200 words to 500, do it. If the article needs to be submitted next Friday, meet the deadline.

10 **Be fresh.** Make your style lively and fresh, preferring the active voice to the passive, the tangible to the abstract, the use of real examples to vague descriptions. Keep your attention focused on the reader, seeking to inform and entertain.

11   **Edit to perfection.** The popular press demands a writing style which is concise and jargon free. Give your final draft to as many people as possible, accepting constructive criticism with good grace. Above all, respect and accept final direction from the editor. There is no better way to become a better writer than to practise – and the exercise of writing for the popular press ensures practice comes close to perfection.

15

Conference proceedings

Presenting a conference paper is an ideal way to ensure that your research will be written up and offered to the right target audience. The conference may be refereed or not, but either way the definition of an end point, the need to focus on the audience, and the feedback you will receive on the spot will help your paper's route to successful publication.

1   **Understand the 'Call for Papers'.** These notices are well considered, finely tuned communications to be closely read and analysed. Conference organizers are specialists in their field, knowing exactly who should come and what they want to find out. If they want papers about new teamwork practices in hospitals, don't bother them with your research about new financial management techniques for hospital accountants.

2   **Set your objectives.** Why do you want to write the paper and present it in person? Apart from the attraction of travel, most people agree that a conference allows them a unique opportunity to meet colleagues and peers. The questions you will be asked and subsequent discussions about your research will enrich it considerably.

3   **Respond with your abstract.** Preliminary notices give clear outlines about what they want at an early stage – usually an abstract of the paper and some information about yourself. Pay attention to: the purpose, the argument and the implications.

4   **Negotiate the terms.** You will never part with the intellectual ownership of your work (see Chapter 5), but you need to make sure who will assume responsibility for the paper's publication. Most conferences will insist that the paper be included in the conference proceedings and others will offer inclusion in a special issue of a journal. You may want to reserve the right to amend your paper and publish it elsewhere after the conference.

5   **Imagine who will be listening.** Conference papers are presented in person in front of a group of other people. This may seem obvious, but it eludes many presenters who think it's sufficient to stand at a podium and monotonously read their 5000 words to a weary audience. Picture your people as you write your paper.

6   **Stick to the structure.** Every successful presentation follows the same simple adage: 'tell 'em what you're going to say, tell 'em, tell 'em what you told 'em'.

7   **Choose only a few key points.** Looking back at your abstract, construct your paper to cover clearly and chronologically the purpose of your paper, the salient points of the argument and the implications. You will never be able to do justice to all of your material on one conference paper and presentation, so ensure you focus on only the key points of most relevance to your audience.

8   **Use your key points as slides.** Rather than show a slide filled with words, create only a few slides of only a few key points at a time. This will help your audience focus and help you to remain on track during your presentation.

9   **Use strong visual aids.** The paper may include detailed tables and diagrams, but rarely will these be suitable for projection at a conference. Complex tables can be broken down into separate tables, and diagrams should be presented with as few graphic embellishments as possible.

10   **Leave time for questions.** If you find yourself running short of time, end your presentation early rather than risk not having time for questions or feedback. This is the most useful benefit you'll receive from the conference, so don't sell yourself short.

11   **Apply what you've learned.** Although your conference paper may already be published in the proceedings, the questions and insights you'll take home with you should help you take your thinking one stage further. Revise your paper accordingly and consider submitting it to a journal (see Chapter 4).

16

Journals

Journals are the right publication to target for specific purposes of dissemination to an academic or professional audience. Their standards are specific and rigorous, and the benefits are not commercial but prestigious. Deciding to follow a journals route requires a thorough evaluation of the process and pitfalls. Here are some points which may help you to establish your criteria.

1   **Think quality not quantity.** A journal has a lower circulation than a magazine or newspaper. Your article might indeed be read by the 'right' people, but don't expect widespread popularity. You can, of course, decide to write your research up for a further, wider target audience as well.

2   **Speed is not of the essence.** Full-length papers may take anywhere from three months to two years to be published. Cultivate patience rather than expect early results. If it is important that your work gets published quickly, for example, if you know of some competing research that is hot on your tail, you may wish to re-think whether a top journal is your target.

3   **Impact values count.** Depending on your speciality, you may be restricted in your choice of the 'top journals'. While we encourage you to widen your potential sources, there may be pressure from your institution or sponsors to only appear in the most notable publications. And that's a crowded space!

4   **Personal creativity is discouraged.** Journals exist to disseminate knowledge to a learned audience and are therefore obliged to set and maintain standards. Your personal preference for style or approach will not be as important as your ability to adhere to guidelines.

5   **Academics are inefficient publishers.** Get used to experiencing delays in communication and longer lead times than you would have thought possible. Many authors despair at the bureaucracy and inefficient nature of academic publishing – but that tends to be its nature. See 2 above.

6   **Yes, there is an 'old-boy network'.** While you would be incorrect in assuming that papers get published because authors are friends of the editor, academe is a tightly knit and well established community of researchers and reviewers. Relationships won't determine success or failure, but they count.

7   **Change happens slowly.** If your work challenges the established thinking of the journal, you must be prepared to have every detail and phrase examined microscopically. Some journals go out of their way to develop counter-intuitive perspectives, but others may tend to reinforce the *status quo*.

8   **Feedback is patchy.** It's encouraging for an author to receive constructive feedback, even if a paper is rejected, but many journal editors and reviewers simply don't have the time. It can be disheartening to receive a curt 'no' after waiting months for a response.

9   **Publication means recognition.** Despite the sometimes irksome nature of academic publishing, having your paper published will lend great weight to your work and to your institution. Although the community may be fairly closed, publication can open many new doors.

10   **Practice makes perfect.** By the time you have endured the difficult and sometimes frustrating process of paper preparation, review and publication you will find it much easier to do it all again the next time. The experience will help you to perfect some very useful disciplines.

17

Edited collections

Editing a book is a bit like a woman having a baby. Often you don't quite know how you got talked into it, it proves to be a long and arduous process, it seems to take over your life completely, bits of it are far more painful than you would have believed possible, you often swear you will never do it again and yet the outcome is a source of delight on arrival! These tips are designed to help you glide through the process serenely (or at least survive it)!

1   **Don't underestimate the amount of time editing a collection of chapters can take**. Editing other people's work is slower than writing it yourself, especially when people fail to respond to your urgent pleas for clarification, explanation or additional detail. However, it is a wonderfully developmental process as it ensures that you are reading in detail much current and interesting work.

2   **Produce a checklist for your authors.** For example, let them know what system you want them to use for references, how you want the text laid out, what system you want to use with headings and sub-headings, what word limits you are putting on the chapters and so on.

3   **Consider putting together a model chapter.** This can be a way of letting your authors know not only about the conventions to be used in the collection, but also to give them an idea of the style and tone of writing expected from them. Be careful, however, not to make the model chapter turn into a straightjacket which could impede contributors' own flair and styles.

4   **Work out in advance how you are going to select your contributors.** To make editing a meaningful process, you need to provide a clear editorial steer. This starts with clarifying the nature, scope and style of the chapters you are looking for. You need to think about how academic you expect the work to be, what proportion of diagrams, graphs and pictures you want to use and the kind of authorial voice you expect from your authors.

5   **Devise a system of quality control and be frank with your contributors.** Many edited books suffer from unevenness in quality, as evidenced in reviews of them. To ensure that all contributions are of high quality, and on theme, tell the authors that the first manuscript will be quality controlled, and will be returned for refinement as a matter of course.

6   **Think about the balance of your material.** You may perhaps wish to include young unknown authors alongside more established writers. It is important to work out to what extent the book will be theoretical, practical or both. How far will it relate to established knowledge and research and how much will it break new ground? Will it provide a single unified perspective or will a number of views be included?

7   **Decide how you are going to manage the process.** How hands-on are you going to be? Will you check and modify every sentence of your authors' writing, will you ask them to do extensive rewriting to your suggestions or will you include it more or less as it is written? If you work extensively on the text, at what stage will you discuss this with the original author? Will you send chapter proofs to each author or are you solely responsible?

8   **Make sure you can easily contact your chapter authors.** Ask them not only for work addresses, fax numbers and e-mail but also for home details, where messages can be left, and so on. When you urgently need the original of a diagram, or missing references, it is a nuisance not to be able to get hold of them.

9   **Be realistic with your deadlines.** People normally take longer to get back to you than you would think possible. A fax marked 'urgent' with a request for immediate response normally results in action (when the author receives it), while letters and phone calls are easier to ignore.

10 **Consider using e-mail.** Never rely entirely on e-mail as this is still an unreliable medium and not everyone has access to it. Be cautious particularly about relying on text sent as attachments as these are currently notoriously problematic. If you want to use e-mail, and most of your contributors have access to it, try sending a short word-processed file of little consequence around your contributors, and check how best to ensure that all or most of them can both read it and edit it.

11 **Do whatever you can to make text management easy.** It is enormously helpful (and almost unheard of) to persuade all your authors to use compatible wordprocessing formats and to supply everything on disk in forms that you can read. A few basic guidelines, such as asking authors to provide text as ASCII or Rich Text Format files can help.

12   **Allow plenty of time for the later stages.** Compiling an index for work written by others is often a complex and demanding task, even if you use appropriate software. It also takes additional time to manage the process of letting authors check the proofs of the individual chapters, if this is what has been agreed.

13   **Make sure you get the names and designations right when you compile the list of contributors.** People get very touchy if you get these sorts of details wrong, and designations, titles and even names may change over the course of the editing process.

18

Selecting papers for publication

An editor's role is to ensure that all papers published in his or her publication reflect the editorial objectives of the publication and therefore the needs of its readers. We're assuming that the publication's objectives are clear and available to prospective authors. The editor must also take responsibility for the final version of the paper, and will often work with authors on revisions. Here are the stages in the selection process most editors go through.

1   **Can this paper survive the five-minute test?** Editors may receive hundreds of papers each week. It wouldn't be possible to read and fully understand each paper just to make a judgement about its suitability for the publication. A fast, foolproof method is required. A quick five-minute scan should reveal whether the paper meets the necessary criteria.

2   **Is the purpose clear?** Has the author clearly stated the purpose within the first few paragraphs? Can you be sure what the purpose is in less than a minute of reading time? If not, it is unlikely the author has the clarity of thinking necessary to carry the paper along.

3   **Does the author's purpose match the purpose of the publication?** Someone may submit a fascinating theoretical paper on quantum physics, but if your publication exists to show young people how to conduct useful experiments at home, you won't be interested.

4   **Can you identify key points quickly?** You should be able to tell in just a few moments what the paper is about. A well-structured paper has sub-headings which help the reader follow the flow, and summarizes at key intervals to help reinforce understanding.

5 **Do the key points support the purpose?** Can the author retain focus, or does the paper drift off onto interesting but irrelevant tangents? Some authors may be trying to pare down a weighty work into just a few pages – do they demonstrate the skill of being able to work within those limitations?

6 **Do you know why the paper is important?** The author shouldn't be leaving you guessing about the paper's significance. The implications, or 'so what' values of the paper should strike you clearly. If an author hasn't done this, chances are he or she hasn't really thought it through – or maybe the paper isn't important.

7 **Is it readable?** Has it been difficult for you to understand what the author means? If you, who are accustomed to reading hundreds of papers, can't understand it, how will your readers? You may choose to confer with the author about his or her literacy, but it would be easier to wait for a better writer to come along and tackle the same subject.

8 **Does it follow your housestyle?** Authors who present papers in a style which doesn't match your publication's are not serious about publishing with you. They are the kinds of authors who send their papers to different publications at random – and you may be the last on their list. Unless you're desperate, work with authors who show they are keen to work with you.

9 **Will it make a lot of work for you?** If you feel you may need to do a great deal of editorial work on a paper, you may need to question whether it is worth your time and effort. Is the proposed contribution so unique, so authoritative and so relevant that you must take it seriously?

10 **Will the authors deliver?** It's more dependable to work with experienced authors, but newcomers deserve a chance, too. Before pinning all your hopes on a revised paper coming back to you in the right shape and on time, ask the author to respond much earlier than you really need it. Most experienced editors will tell you – 10 promises equals one paper.

19

Communication matters

Most people find that problems start when one party doesn't understand what the other is saying. Editors, reviewers and authors are no different – although one might think that specialists in communication would be above such problems. Effective communication is a discipline. Here are some suggestions to editors for getting it, and keeping it flowing.

1   **Put everything in writing.** What we say can be misinterpreted, written down haphazardly or even completely forgotten. It's far easier, and more foolproof, to write a few paragraphs or even a checklist of items. With e-mail and faxes, the written word takes less time to communicate than the spoken word.

2   **But don't forget the warmth of a human voice.** Having noted the tip above, remember how nice it is to hear the voice of the person with whom you are working. Don't be afraid to follow up a letter or e-mail with a telephone call. Even long distance charges are cheap compared to the benefit of deepening a working relationship.

3   **Acknowledge everything.** Rarely will an editor decide about a paper the moment it arrives. While it may take days or weeks before a decision can be communicated to the author, a standard letter of acknowledgement can be sent immediately.

4   **Manage the 'black holes'.** Journal publishing outfits can be very inefficient. Perhaps being surrounded by so many interesting papers makes daily operational challenges that much less interesting. Don't assume silence is golden – the paper may be lost or forgotten. Remind people.

5   **Be constructive.** Editors and their advisors wield enormous power as they feed back to authors their comments and suggestions. But they sometimes lapse into terse language, neglecting to wrap their criticism in something palatable. Authors who receive unfriendly responses must learn to swallow hard and put it down to bad manners.

6   **Ask questions sooner rather than later.** If you receive suggestions from a reviewer or author that you don't understand, seek clarification as soon as possible. It won't be an acceptable excuse to phone or fax just before the deadline saying something was unclear. Take responsibility for clarifying understanding.

7   **Communicate the bad news, too.** No news is good news wasn't an expression generated in the publishing industry. No news could be terrible news – like the reviewer we sent your paper to can't be found, or the disk that you sent us is corrupted so someone in IT is trying to figure it out, or the paperclips didn't hold and we're still looking for your introduction. Tell people that everything has slowed down because there's a problem. Who knows – maybe they can help.

8   **Copy everybody.** Publishing is always an inter-related communication event. There are always several people involved in any one step of the process. It's far easier to copy everybody involved than to leave someone out and have to backtrack.

9   **Say thank you.** Many first time authors are so nervous about being rejected that they forget they're doing the editor and publisher a favour. Authors certainly aren't in the business of writing for money; saying 'thank you' and 'well done' is a small gesture, but one most authors take to heart warmly.

10   **Ask for more.** One good author is worth ten mediocre ones. If you've enjoyed working with someone and liked their work, invite them to work with you again. Don't take it for granted that you will be their next first choice.

Chapter 3   Writing books

20   Targeting a publishing company
21   Getting an overview
22   Using information sources effectively
23   Guidelines on proposal contents
24   Writing a good proposal
25   Book proposal timescales
26   Thinking about the international dimension
27   Establishing a market for your book
28   Marketing your book
29   Working with your publisher
30   Publication dates and launches
31   Book contracts
32   Money matters

This chapter is mainly concerned with writing books, but many of the topics and issues we include also relate to other types of publication, too. A particular emphasis throughout this chapter is establishing a good working relationship with your prospective publisher, and making sure that this collaboration serves both parties well.

We start with some suggestions about 'Targeting a publishing company', and offer some advice to help you find the best publisher for your proposed work. 'Getting an overview' is extremely important in any kind of writing, and it is useful to spend some time achieving this before you expect anyone else to be in a position to make valid decisions on whether or not to accept and publish your work.

To get started on writing something as big as a book, even if you are co-authoring it, rather than writing it alone, will entail marshalling a lot of information first. We offer some advice on time efficient ways of going about this.

We continue this chapter with three sets of suggestions about writing book proposals for publishers. Writing a proposal is a make or break affair. If your proposal is successful, you will be contracted to go ahead with your writing. If not, you may feel that no-one will ever publish your work, but this need not necessarily be the case. There is a lot you can do both to make sure that your proposal is a good one, and that it gets sent to the most appropriate publisher and has maximum impact when it gets there.

The next three topics are 'Thinking about the international dimension', 'Establishing a market for your book' and actually 'Marketing your book'. You may at first glance think 'why should I concern myself with such things; is that not someone else's job?' However, anticipating these aspects of the publication of your work, and building them into your proposal, will help to ensure that your work is published, and reaches the most relevant audiences.

We conclude this chapter with four related matters: 'Working with your publisher', 'Publication dates and launches', 'Book contracts' and 'Money matters'. Although you may feel that these things are a long way from the business of writing, they are very close to the business of getting published. Doing your part well in all of these things can help endear you to your publisher, and can open up the way to further writing opportunities.

20

Targeting a publishing company

Although at the outset, the prospect of having your book published at all, by anyone, may feel very exciting, you need to target your publishing company carefully. You need to do all that you can to ensure that you get the best company for your proposed book. The overall size of the company is less important than presence or strengths in the particular field or subject area. You are looking for the company which will be best placed to sell the greatest quantities of your book. Think ahead to how your book might be sold – in bookshops, by direct mail, in your own country, and possibly worldwide. The following suggestions may help you find the publisher that will serve your purposes best.

1 **Research carefully, and make a list of publishers to contact.** You will probably already have a good idea of which publishers to think about. They will be the ones who publish the books you read in your subject area. Even so, it is worth doing some research to find out which publishers have active future publishing programmes embracing your discipline area.

2 **Decide which companies have the strongest market presence.** Find out which companies have good quantities of their relevant titles in the target sections of bookshops. Check out which companies regularly have stands at conferences or exhibitions you visit. Which companies send regular mailings to you or to your colleagues?

3 **Ask friends or colleagues for their recommendations.** If you know people who have had books published, discuss with them their experiences with publishers. Ask about which publishers have proved to be reliable, and which communicated regularly during the writing stages. Ask how long they took to publish from manuscript stage, and how well they have marketed the books. Find out as much as you can about each publisher.

4 **Draw up a shortlist of companies in the order that you will approach them.** Your research should help you to decide which publishers may be most suitable for your book. List them in order of your preference.

5 **Decide whether or not to submit multiple proposals simultaneously.** If your book topic is time sensitive, it may help to speed up the process to send a proposal to each company on your list at the same time. However, it is only fair to mention to each publisher in your letter that you are approaching the other companies. Commissioning editors from companies talk to each other, and don't like to find out that authors are secretly approaching several companies at a time!

6 **Make it easy for each publisher to contact you.** Give clear home and work address details, and confirm which you prefer the publisher to use. Include phone, fax and e-mail details where you can, but *only* include channels of communication which really work on an everyday basis. A potential publisher may well want to contact you urgently to clarify something in your proposal, and could soon lose interest if unable to get an immediate response from you. At the very least, include an address or phone number from which urgent messages will be passed on to you wherever you are.

7 **Don't send your proposal to 'Dear Sir or Madam…'.** Proposals submitted in this way (or worse, to 'Dear Sir…' only) create a poor first impression. Such submissions show that authors have not been thorough in their background research. Such proposals are treated slowly, too, as editors tend to shuffle them around internally. They may take longer to reach the desk of the most appropriate editor, or may never reach it.

8 **Send your proposal to a named individual at each company.** Find out the name of the commissioning editor responsible for your subject area in each of your chosen companies. The surest way of doing this is to ring up each company, and ask the receptionist for the name of the commissioning editor in your field.

9 **Don't send letters or proposals that are obviously photocopied.** If you are sending out multiple copies, you should still address each letter to a particular commissioning editor by name, and make it relevant to that particular publisher. For example, you may wish to suggest to one company that your book could be published in its 'Tourism Management' list, while for another publisher it could be the 'Recreation and Leisure' list. Print out fresh copies of the proposal itself, preferably with further adjustments as suggested below.

10 **Tweak your proposal to suit each publishing company.** Make minor modifications to the synopsis of your proposal, specifying which precise series or list you see as the potential home for your book. In the 'Competition' section of your proposal, clarify how your proposed book will complement the nearest similar book on the publisher's list.

21

Getting an overview

If you are writing a book you will normally have gone through the stages of producing some kind of overview or synopsis as part of your proposal to your publisher. For example, you may have listed indicative contents or chapter titles. However, it is worth doing some further brainstorming of your ideas before you really get down to writing. The following suggestions may help you to create a useful map of your proposed work, and may stop you wasting a lot of time going off on tangents.

1   **Take a blank sheet of paper and write your working title in a box in the middle.** It does not matter at this stage if you're likely to change the title. This could be the start of a map of your book, and more importantly, it is that crucial stage without which nothing happens: a start!

2   **Brainstorm your key ideas onto paper.** Draw spokes radiating out from the box with your title in it, one at a time, adding the main keywords for each idea or area that you may wish to cover at the end of each spoke. You may like to do this with the aid of the indicative content that you may already have supplied to your publisher, or you may like to rethink the content afresh, then go back to compare with your original intentions.

3   **Keep looking back at your title as you brainstorm your ideas.** This is to make sure that you don't get carried away with second order ideas, or tangents. All of the main keywords at the end of the spokes should be important ones, and all clearly deriving from the title.

4   **Flesh out your keyword ideas.** You may like to do this after you've generated most of your main ideas, or one at a time as you think of each idea. Find out which works best for you. Keep to key words or phrases, however, and resist for the present the temptation to compose sentences or paragraphs. The main reason why it's worth fleshing out your ideas at this stage is so that you don't lose important thoughts that may go through your mind as you are brainstorming the content of your writing.

5   **Think about doing a parallel, or separate, brainstorm of the work you intend to refer to.** It can be useful to go through your ideas' brainstorm, adding in a different colour the names and dates of the main books, papers or articles that will be central references in due course. At this stage, don't aim for these to be complete; you can still add or delete as your writing proceeds.

6   **Start sequencing your ideas.** Stand back from the map which is emerging of the content of your proposed writing, and look for where, on your map, is the most sensible place to lead in. In another colour, write a number one against this idea. Then look for what follows on most logically from this point; it may well not be an adjacent point on your map. Put a number two beside that idea. Continue in this way.

7   **Look for where is going to be the best place to finish.** Work out which ideas you wish to save for the end, so that your writing comes to a strong conclusion. Put an 'X' beside this idea, to remind you to use it as your exit point.

8   **Keep this overview as a working document.** Don't regard it as finished. Use it frequently to review what the overall shape of your piece will be, and add in fresh keywords and supporting ideas whenever you really need to (even if this will mean going back and working them into material that by then you have already written).

9   **Carry your overview around with you.** Maybe make one or two extra copies, so that you've got one pinned up where you do most of your writing, and another with you at most times. This allows you to keep in your mind the overall shape of your writing, and to make alterations when something new or important occurs to you.

10   **Relate your overview to the target word count.** If you are to work within an agreed length, you will need to establish early on in the writing process approximately how many words you have available for each of your main ideas. This could save you from a lot of editing work later, and help you to write succinctly right from the start, rather than go to excessive length on your first main ideas.

22

Using information sources effectively

Most writers admit that the problem today is not with the availability of information, but with its profusion. People are writing books and articles about everything. A simple search can turn into a logistical nightmare unless you have a clear plan to guide you. The following tips are designed to help you plan your best information searching strategy.

1   **Create a plan of known likely sources.** Before you begin to look for information, decide how you will do it. Write a list of likely sources and where they can be found. You'll find this step will help you to remain more focused and less open to distraction.

2   **Decide what you're really looking for.** Make lists of keywords that relate to the sources you already know, including authors' names as well as topic descriptors. Check for alternative words or phrases, meaning the same thing, that occur in different sources that you already know.

3   **Narrow your focus.** A search on 'strategic planning' will yield hundreds of thousands of books and papers. Make sure you define your topic as precisely and narrowly as possible. You should be doing this anyway at the beginning of your research and writing project.

4   **Start with the obvious.** Most literature draws on previous contributors to the field. If you want to gain a good basic grounding, go right to the sources. You can always follow through with a later tangent when you know how your work is becoming further refined.

5 **Talk to the librarian.** Unless you're a career academic, you may not be fully aware of how a modern library works. Libraries are staffed by information professionals whose job encompasses not only an understanding of their collections, but a firm grasp of the research and information retrieval business. Just explain what you're interested in and you'll find that most librarians will become enthusiastic participants in your search.

6 **Learn to use a citation index.** Now that you've read up on some of the seminal works in your field, a citation index will tell you how the primary authors are used in the work of others. This is where you'll see that author A significantly informed the work of author B whose papers were criticized but largely upheld by author C until author D discredited most of the earlier work through ground breaking research.

7 **Access secondary sources.** Secondary sources review and publish abstracts from a wide variety of journals and books in a particular field. The source may be selective or comprehensive. Test out such secondary sources by trying to look in them for some key publications you already know about. If they don't deliver the goods you know about, they may not be too good for finding the ones you don't yet know about!

8 **Try news agencies and clipping services.** For a reasonable fee you can subscribe to a service which will scan and clip relevant articles according to your prescribed criteria.

9 **Experiment with online searches.** Covered more fully in a later chapter, online searching is fast, but inefficient unless you can narrow your topic to just a few possibilities.

10 **Enjoy some return on your taxes.** Most government agencies or bodies are willing – and often required – to help you access relevant information. Trade councils, export boards and other government departments will often be able to supply you with detailed information. It may take some time to find the most relevant departments, or the right people in such departments, so start your searches early.

11 **Approach organizations directly.** Most organizations have communication departments who will give you information about their organization and often the industry or community sector in which they operate.

23

Guidelines on proposal contents

It is usually sensible to have a book proposal accepted before writing any non-fiction book, and you should start the process by providing a book proposal. Most publishers will need information covering the same general areas, and it is a good idea to discuss these in advance. Listed below are tips on the basic information any publisher will need on your book before making a decision whether to accept it or not.

1   **Ask the publisher you are approaching for 'house' guidelines on submitting a proposal.** Ring the publisher and ask an editor to send you any notes for authors and editors they may have prepared. This means that you can be sure of covering all the points of information needed by them from the outset.

2   **Name your book.** Self-evidently your work will need a working title, even if this subsequently changes several times. The title should indicate the scope of the book and should be as informative and as succinct as possible. Don't go for anything gimmicky or mysterious: commissioning editors tend to fight shy of these.

3   **Draw up a contents list.** A provisional list of chapter headings is normally needed, together with a couple of sentences summarizing what each chapter will contain to give a feel for the content. This will help editors to decide whether it is the right kind of book for them.

4   **Give a brief synopsis of the book.** This is where you can outline which areas you will examine, your reasons for writing it and what style and approach you plan. Be sure to emphasize any key or unique features of the book. If, for example, you plan to include case studies and checklists at the end of each chapter, you should indicate these here.

5   **Identify the market for your book.** Be as specific as you can in your description of the audience you have in mind. State the level of the readers you have in mind and how many there are likely to be. Provide some approximate data, giving , for example approximate numbers of university departments that study the area you are writing about if this is an academic text. Outline the potential you see for international sales.

6   **Outline the competition.** Cite the nearest competing published titles that you have found. This is usually preferable in a publisher's eyes to saying you have found no existing competition, which may suggest you don't know your field very well. Give details of publisher, price, author, format, and ISBN if you can.

7   **State why your book is different and/or better than the competition.** However, proceed with caution! It is not impossible that the person who is asked by your publisher to review your proposal is the author of a competing text, so it is unwise to trash it.

8   **Provide the author's biographical details.** One or two paragraphs is what is needed here rather than a full CV to plough through. You should include details of present or recent employment where appropriate, together with membership of any societies or associations that may be relevant to the book.

9   **Convince the publisher you can do it.** Give details of any previous published work, so that they can see that you can deliver the goods. This doesn't have to be just full scale, commercially published material: in-house publications for example can also indicate you know how to write to brief and to deadlines. If you haven't published yet, give information about relevant research or professional experience that will underpin your book.

10   **Provide one or more sample chapters.** Many publishers feel this is the best way to get a sense of the way you write. Don't worry about over-committing yourself at this stage. It is accepted that the sample chapter may appear in the final book in a very different form. But it is worth putting a lot of effort into making it as good as possible.

11   **Indicate the length of the manuscript.** Outline the length of the book you plan to write and be as accurate as possible. Identify this either by an approximate word count, or by the number of pages you expect it to run to in a given format. Look at other books similar to the kind you wish to write and use them to help you gauge the right length, or simply multiply the number of chapters by the length of a sample chapter you write.

12 **Try to be as accurate as possible in estimating length.** This will be one of the factors that will determine the selling price of the book and mistakes are expensive. If in doubt, err on the generous side. Your publisher will prefer you to do this than come in with a manuscript that is wildly over-length.

13 **Identify the delivery date.** Realism is the key here too. The planned delivery date should be a commitment, not a pious hope. When a publisher accepts a proposal, the marketing operation may well swing into action fairly quickly. The original delivery date may change by negotiation once the contents are determined, but the publisher needs to know whether to allow months or years before completion.

14 **Always allow yourself a little longer than you think you will need**. Publishers are often able to work around early delivery but hate having to cope with late ones, since catalogues are often printed in advance of completion, and it is administratively complex having to deal with orders for books that are late in getting published. For academic books, a delay of even a few weeks may lead to the loss of a full academic year, for example, when producing a textbook which should not come out mid-term.

15 **Specify the manuscript format you will provide**. Try to be as flexible as possible, as some publishers will only accept text in an agreed word-processing format as well as hard copy. No publisher will accept handwritten material, however good. If you can supply good Camera-Ready Copy, this can be attractive as it saves typesetting costs but this is not normally required. You are normally expected to supply tables and so on as CRC.

24

Writing a good proposal

If you are ever to get the chance to get your book published, then it is essential that you write a really good proposal. Even if you have completed the entire manuscript, a publisher will usually request that only a proposal be sent initially. View the proposal as a sales vehicle for your masterpiece and try to include a mention of all its key features.

1   **Follow the publishers guidelines.** If you received any notes from your chosen publisher on the proposed proposal format, then stick to them. Provide information on each of the areas listed in the guidelines and don't leave any out.

2   **Give information on all the areas listed in the Guidelines on Proposals Contents section.** If you are not following specific guidelines, make sure you cover everything that is needed fully, and use the broad areas indicated as sub-headings for your proposal.

3   **Use the proposal as a sales tool for your book.** This is the vehicle that will help you to secure a contract for your book, so you need to really polish it. Emphasize its unique and key selling points strongly and make sure that the proposal sounds interesting enough to make the editor feel it will make a good book.

4   **Research your targeted publisher's lists.** Get catalogues from the publishers you plan to target and research which series, if any, your book might fit into. Publishers tend to group the books they publish into lists or series that they can market together. There's no point trying to publish with a publisher who doesn't normally market books in your area of work.

5   **Indicate where your book would fit on your publisher's list.** State in your synopsis which list (or specific series) you see accommodating your book. Explain why you see it sitting alongside other books in the series and how your book would complement them.

6   **Keep the proposal brief.** A proposal should normally be fairly concise, running to up to four sheets of A4 paper or so typed in single spacing. Of course, it will take more pages if it is attractively laid out using headings and sub-headings for emphasis.

7   **Get feedback on your proposal.** Once your proposal is drafted, ask one or two people to read it over. These need not be experts in your discipline as their function is to give comments on the overall shape of the proposal. They may also spot typographical and other errors that you have missed, that would otherwise give a poor impression of your work. They can also confirm that it is crystal clear to someone reading it with a fresh eye. If they identify queries or problems, these can be reviewed and resolved before you make an actual submission.

8   **Submit a clear, clean document.** Make sure that the proposal is printed out freshly, is well laid out and is a clean copy. Leave generous margins around the edges so it doesn't look cramped. If you spot an error or make a last minute amendment, correct it on the disk and make another copy. Remember that a scruffy, badly presented proposal bodes ill for a good working relationship with a publisher.

9   **Put the title and your name as a footer or header clearly on each sheet.** Number pages clearly and make sure that each sheet is identifiable in case of a mix up when your publisher photocopies it.

10   **Write a letter to accompany the proposal.** A good letter is important. It is worth finding out the name of the commissioning editor and writing a personalized letter to a named person explaining why you have sent it there. Use the letter to sell your proposal and to outline the general subject area on which your proposal focuses. Also, let the publisher know if you have sent out copies of the proposal simultaneously to other publishing houses. In any case, limit the mail shot to only a handful of the most likely publishers.

25

Book proposal timescales

Writing a book takes time. It may be harder than you think to work out some of the timescales that can be involved. The suggestions below will help you to plan your book proposal with timescales that will be attainable and reasonable.

1 **Allow yourself plenty of time to research your book idea.** You could need several weeks to carry out the background research on which to base a proposal before starting to write it. You may well have to do this work alongside everything else in your life, so it could take quite a long time.

2 **Don't rush in to writing a proposal.** Your proposal is the basis of a selling tool for marketing your book, so it is your proposal that will win or lose you a contract. Write your proposal slowly and carefully.

3 **Try to calculate approximately how many hours it may take to write the book.** Whatever figure you come up with, add on at least half again for good measure, especially if it is your first book! Other authors will confirm that it usually takes a lot longer than one thinks.

4 **Look objectively at your personal circumstance for the year ahead.** Take account of any big events which are looming up, such as house moves, a new baby, or a possible job change. Such events invariably eat into any time planned for writing. Decide what seems to be an attainable number of hours per month that you could build up around all these possibilities. Err on the cautious side in your calculations!

5 **Divide the total time estimate by the monthly total you should be able to manage.** This will give you an estimate of how many months the book should take.

6   **Think about the 'life expectancy' of the topic you are going to write on.** Compare this with your calculations, and be prepared for a shock if you are thinking of writing on a rapidly changing subject, or in an area where a significant new development is already visible on the horizon (for example, a change in legislation). You may have to be prepared to rethink your whole strategy if you find that it will be crucial to have the book finished by an earlier deadline because of outside events in the field in which you're writing.

7   **Think carefully before you propose a deadline for manuscript completion.** Proposals usually require you to give such a deadline, but take into account your estimates before you commit yourself. Six months ahead can seem a long time when enthusiasm is high to get started. For a busy person, there can be surprisingly few available days in six months.

8   **State your delivery date as '… months after offer of a contract'.** It's unwise to start work on the book until you have secured a contract. Any one publisher may take three months or more to accept and reject your proposal, and will send it out to other people in your field for review comments. You may also be thinking of approaching more than one publisher, and waiting to see if you have rival contract offers to weigh up.

9   **Once completed, leave your proposal aside for a few days.** However tempting it is to rush along to the post box and get it on its way, don't! Look at it again with a fresh eye to check for errors, and think how it reads to an 'outsider' who has no more than what is written there to make a decision on your book.

10   **Get informal feedback on your proposal before you send it to your publisher.** Build in time for others to review your proposal. Although it may not take you long to write a proposal once you've done your research, you will still need to give the friends and colleagues who look at your draft proposal at least a week to read your proposal and to get their comments and suggestions back to you.

26

Thinking about the international dimension

At the proposal stage, it is important to settle the international issues which may be involved in your writing. If your book is to cover a topic that is of interest only to a home market, confirm this so that you can aim at this audience. If, however, the subject could have wider sales potential, be sure to emphasize this at the proposal stage, and do what you can to include wider frames of reference bearing international readers in mind. The following suggestions may help your proposal to be seen to reach a wider audience.

1   **Decide whether the content is focused in your home country or is international.** Establish at an early stage whether your subject will be given a treatment appropriate to a home audience or an international one. Work out whether you will draw only, or mainly, on local data, facts and examples, or whether you will bring in data from other countries.

2   **Decide where the book is likely to sell.** Work out whether the specific audiences you plan to write for are home based or international. For example, think about whether your book may interest cross sections of the population in areas such as USA, Canada, Australia and Europe, and whether similar target audiences in any, or all, of such parts of the world may be just as likely to gain something from your proposed work.

3   **Make your content accessible to international readers.** When your content will be relevant to readers in several countries, avoid using jargon or acronyms specific to one country or, when you must use them, explain them clearly. Make reference to parallel examples and instances from other countries as often as possible.

4   **Be aware of your publisher's international sales network.** Most publishing companies have lists of international agents and operate through representatives around the world, even when they don't have offices of their own in other countries.

5   **Pave the way for your publisher's agents to sell your work.** Unless a book is completely home-country oriented, publishers' agents will try to sell it elsewhere. Help them by passing on to your editor any specific contacts you have in other countries. For example, if you have worked in other countries, put details of such contacts on the 'Author Questionnaire' you are likely to get from your publisher.

6   **Make the most of any work you do in other countries.** If you visit other countries to work, find out about what is available in print there in your subject area, and which publishers are most directly relevant. Such information can be of value to your own publisher when considering how to promote your work in other countries.

7   **Think about possibilities of translation into other languages.** Let your publisher know if you are aware of any significant possibilities that could justify your work being translated. If you have already had your work translated into other languages, give details to your publisher.

8   **Increase the chance of a co-publishing arrangement.** If the international context and relevance is clarified at the outset in your book, particularly in the introduction, it is more likely to lead to publishers in other countries being willing to co-publish with your own publisher.

9   **Be careful with your language and wording.** Attention to small details can increase international possibilities, such as when UK authors use 'z' spellings rather than 's' spellings so that their work is seen to lend itself to US publishing. Words like 'overseas' are peculiar to people living on islands, and are best avoided in your quest for an international reputation.

10   **Don't underestimate the potential benefits to *you* of publishing internationally.** These include getting the opportunities to visit and work in countries you may not have dreamed about.

27

Establishing a market for your book

Our suggestions here include tips to help you to decide what commercial market might exist for your book, and about deciding which market or audience you will be addressing as the readers of your work. You will need to be clear on both counts before starting to write, and in your drive to persuade a publisher to take on your book.

1   **Research your book idea.** Once you have come up with an idea for a book, you will need to convince yourself that there is a current need for what you have in mind and that a similar book does not already exist. Discuss your idea with colleagues, look in relevant sections of bookshops and publishers' catalogues, to back up your hunch.

2   **Research the existing competition.** You'll need to be clear on the content and approach of any works which could be seen by others as competition. This will help you to defend your proposal to publishers. You will need to be able to state what is new and unique about your proposal. Check also 'Whitakers Books in Print' (CD-ROM or paper versions in most public or college libraries). Use library catalogues and online databases to see what's already been written, by whom and when.

3   **Decide the details you need to note from each existing book.** These may seem obvious, but remember to include title, author(s), number of pages, year, publisher, place of publication and price. It's worth jotting down the ISBN numbers of important books.

4   **Make a list of competing titles.** Build this up as you do your research into what's available. It's worth jotting down the full details of each important source you discover, as it takes ages to go back and find them out again.

5   **Annotate your list.** Write a sentence or two to capture your thoughts on the individual books. Phrases such as 'very dense', 'too academic', 'doesn't cover thixotropy very well' can help you work out why the book will not really compete with your proposed masterpiece. Price is worth considering too, such as '£35 for 400 pp in hardback won't compete with my £10 paperback of 180 pp'.

6   **Decide what's wrong with the main competition.** In making your proposal to a publisher, you will need to be able to explain how your book will meet needs which the competition (however famous) fails to address. Don't pretend that a serious competitor doesn't exist; publishers send book proposals to reviewers, and are quickly told if there are important competitors that have been ignored in proposals.

7   **What's new about *your* book?** You will need to be able to state what is new and unique about your proposal. How does it go further than existing books? What different angles may it take to books 'x' and 'y'?

8   **Think about the life expectancy of your book.** Will it be focusing on a fast changing field, where a specific short period of sales-life is likely? Or will your pearls of wisdom remain valid for a number of years? Such information will be needed to help you to choose and woo a publisher, and to decide how long a writing period you can allow yourself.

9   **Work out your audience.** Clarify at the outset who will constitute your intended audience. Decide which specific groups within an area you are really writing for. For example, are you addressing undergraduate students on leisure and tourism courses, or practising hotel and restaurant managers? You will need to keep your primary target audience clearly in mind while writing.

10 **Think about who may actually *buy* your book.** Collect any data you can on the numbers involved in different sectors of your audience who will be likely to buy your book. Such data will help you to propose your case to publishers. For example, a book on employment rights might be aimed at the 76,000 members of the Institute of Personnel and Development, and approximately 800 students per year at twelve universities offering human resource management diplomas. Try to work out an estimate of the proportion of the target audience who may end up purchasing their own copies.

28

Marketing your book

Your publisher should be fully committed to maximizing sales of your book, but the vigour with which you add your own marketing can make a substantial difference to sales figures. Take advantage of any opportunities which present themselves, not just for the financial spin-offs, but for the increased recognition which you can gain in your field.

1   **Remember that it is in your own interest to market your book.** Don't be lazy and leave it all to your publisher. Also, don't be too modest. While it is possible to put people off a book by being too marketing-oriented, it is best not to hide your light too firmly under a bushel. It can, for example, be quicker to send flyers and posters out yourself, in mailings you are doing anyway, than to ask your publisher to have copies sent out.

2   **Use your professional networks.** Make sure that your friends and colleagues know about your book and trust them to promote it for you. Sending people flyers or posters can be useful, or get them to take small piles of such papers to conferences or meetings they are attending.

3   **Author marketing groundwork is usually acted upon by publishers.** For example, publishers are usually willing to send flyers to relevant conferences, and maybe even to set up a display stand.

4   **Get to know the marketing people at your publisher.** Find out the names of the marketing executive and sales manager who are promoting your book. They will work all the better for you if they feel they know you. While you may already feel you know people such as commissioning editors, these are not the most relevant people when it comes to getting your book sold.

5   **Feed in marketing information regularly.** Make it a matter of routine to alert your publisher to relevant conferences, new developments in your field that are relevant to your work, and so on.

6   **Always keep at least one display copy.** Put sticky labels on saying 'Display Copy' or 'Not to be taken away' Leaving such copies in a coffee area or on an exhibition stand can be a way of letting people scan your work without the pressure of you watching them do so.

7   **Make your own exhibition.** For example, mount a copy of the cover, and any other relevant display material on your office wall so that visitors are alerted to your work without you having to tell them about it.

8   **Get your own promotional flyer.** Publishers often make these anyway, and will be happy to supply you with a reasonable quantity of these. If not, draft your own design and send it to your publisher for consideration. Remember to make sure that the price, postage charge and publisher's address are all on the flyer. If possible, have a picture of the book cover on the flyer, so that people will know your book when they see it.

9   **Update your promotional flyer.** Add in positive comments from reviews, and update your biographical details when necessary. It can also be worth adding to your flyer a little about any new policies, trends or developments to which your book is relevant.

10 **Make good use of foreign travel.** Check with your publisher about who the local agents are in countries you are visiting on business. Try to contact the agents in advance; they may be pleased to arrange a promotional event, and to secure sufficient copies so that your book will be available at the time of your visit.

29

Working with your publisher

Particularly in the final stages, close communications with your publisher are vital to the success of your work. The following suggestions should help you to adopt a logical and successful approach to the hurdles of dealing with 'Author Queries' and proof-reading.

1   **Get to know your publisher.** It helps a lot if you have had the chance to meet the person with whom you will be liaising as your book goes on its journey towards publication. When you ring up, it's useful to know who to ask for, and even if you can't meet them you can get to know them over the phone. This makes future dealings happier and more productive.

2   **Keep to deadlines, and try to exceed them.** Publishers often are doing promotion and marketing of your forthcoming book well before you've actually written it, so make sure that you do your bit so that it will be ready when it is due.

3   **Send in your final manuscript exactly as your publisher asks for it.** When publishers say 'double-spaced, single sided A4' that's exactly what they mean, as this leaves room for reviewers and copy-editors to write on comments and changes.

4   **Send disk versions, too.** Find out what wordprocessing packages, and which disk formats your publisher can read. It's fairly easy to find someone who can convert any package into anything else; if in doubt find a computing student. One advantage of disk versions is that they save your publisher a great deal of time regarding 'keying in' or scanning. A more important advantage is that you will have far less copy errors to look for when the manuscript gets to proof stage; you will only get your own errors back in fact, and only some of them!

5   **Be brave about the 'Author Queries'.** Don't be surprised to get two or three tightly-typed A4 sheets listing maybe 47 'Queries' that the publisher's readers have made about your work. Some of these will be easy to attend to (such as 'p28 line 12: do you mean 'usually' or 'sometimes', or 'p56 5 lines up: check spelling of Bloxted reference', or 'p93 line 2: 'Martinon' ref not in Biblio').

6   **Answer the 'Author Queries' straight away.** Regard this as an urgent, important job, and drop everything else. Try not to be out of the country when they arrive; if you *are* going to be unavailable, liaise with your publisher so that a suitable time window can be arranged. The reason for the urgency is that by the time you get the 'Author Queries' your 'job' will have been timetabled into production schedules.

7   **Be there when the proofs arrive.** Turn round times for proofs are usually a few days. If your diary is congested, arrange with your publisher a window when you can guarantee the time it will take to deal with your proofs.

8   **Follow proof-reading instructions to the letter.** At this stage, don't make any significant changes or additions unless they are essential. You may well be charged for these. Follow directions such as 'corrections in red' and make sure each correction is clearly visible when just glancing at a page. Also follow instructions such as 'other changes in blue', as these are ones you may have to pay for.

9   **Get someone else to read your proofs as well as yourself.** A problem with reading one's own proofs is that we all see what we *meant*, and not necessarily what we *wrote*, or what the publisher *printed*.

10   **Be prepared to negotiate with your publisher.** You, as author, are presumably expert in your subject area, in writing as well as in how to get your message across. Your publisher, on the other hand, is expert in book design, book production, promotion, marketing, distribution and sales. Ultimately, both you and the publisher are interested in making a profit, not a loss. So work *with* your publisher to get the best overall result. This will probably mean listening to your publisher's judgement on dust covers, book manufacture, and even negotiating the final title for your book.

11   **Keep a copy of the marked-up proofs.** Copying maybe 200 pages is very boring, but proof-reading the whole lot *again* after the marked-up proofs are lost in the post is much more boring! Send the proofs back well wrapped and labelled; if you possibly can, take them there yourself. You will be likely to be rewarded by a cup of coffee and a great deal less anxiety.

30

Publication dates and launches

The publication date of your book will be an exciting and important time. Think ahead to when you, as an author, can actually hold the fruits of your labours in your hands! From the publisher's point of view, the launch and first three months of a book's life are crucial times. The launch date may mark the culmination of sustained publicity and marketing campaigns, and copies will be in bookshops on that date, maybe even worldwide.

1   **Your book is only new once.** It has just one launch or publication date. It is in your interest to work with your publisher, and even to push your publisher, to make sure that your book's arrival is as noteworthy and memorable as it can be.

2   **Confirm when the official publication date will be.** When working out the best date, think about your intended audience or market, and try to make sure it's a good time for likely purchasers. For example, don't publish an academic text at the end of June in the UK. Also, check whether your new book may be directly relevant to an important international conference, and if possible adjust the timescales to enable it to be ready for such an occasion.

3   **Make sure your publisher knows what you're doing in the three months leading up to the publication date.** During this time, it's important that you can be readily contacted by your publisher, and if you're away from home/work, leave the publisher your telephone and fax or e-mail contact details. For example, there could be a journalist wanting to interview you about your book: don't lose such opportunities.

4   **Make time in your own schedule for publicity and launch event work.** For example, it could be useful for you to search out useful mailing lists for your publisher, or to be able to plan in book-signing events. Try to avoid other important meetings which may make you unavailable at this time.

5   **Help your publisher draw up a review copies list.** Remember that there could be 4–6 weeks between arrival of copies and the official launch date. During this time copies may be sent to reviewers, and your suggestions regarding where the book is likely to be well received are always welcomed by your publisher. It also helps to alert your publisher to the newspapers, journals and magazines where your book could be reviewed. It is normal to send 10–20 review copies straight out, and it is important that these are not wasted opportunities.

6   **Help your publisher prepare promotional flyers and/or press releases.** It's important that you contribute to the wording of such publicity materials, not least to ensure that there are no glitches in your name, present post, contact details and so on.

7   **Work out key people who should be sent a free copy.** You will probably already have a list of such people, not least including people who deserve a copy because of the help they may have given you. It is also worth ensuring that key people in your field are alerted to your new book.

8   **Work with your publisher to explore the possibility of a launch event.** Publishers have not normally got much to spend on such an event, but if you can, for example, build a small celebration event into a conference that is already taking place, you may be able to justify the cost of some additional food or drink.

9   **Pave the way at your local bookshop.** Authors are often saddened that they don't see their work on the shelves in their usual bookshop. This is often because they haven't introduced themselves at the shop; most shops are only too pleased to have a local celebrity on their shelves.

10 **Prepare your own news feature on your book.** Send this to your local press, and further afield if you have contacts. Write a short journalistic piece on some aspect of your work, or a point of local interest covered by your book.

11 **Watch your words at a launch event.** You may not know who you are talking to, so be nice to everyone, and don't be tricked into saying anything negative about yourself, your book, your publisher, or your organisation! Be positive and enthusiastic, and you can't go wrong.

31

Book contracts

Once you are offered a contract, you will naturally be excited and delighted. It is surprising how many authors confess to happily signing the contract without reading it through properly or thinking through the implications of all the sub-clauses. While it is true that most publishers offer standard terms and contracts for the vast majority of works they publish (and there is certainly no intention to trick you), a contract is a legally binding document for both parties, so it is important to be clear about what commitments you are making. Therefore, it makes sense to be absolutely clear about the responsibilities and rights the contract is assigning to both parties.

1   **Ask for a copy of the standard contract at the outset.** Most publishers use standard contacts for particular kinds of books, which are normally based on previous experiences and their knowledge of the sales performance of books on similar subjects aimed at the same market. Various publishers' contracts may look very different, but in general they cover all the same areas.

2   **Familiarize yourself with the kinds of terms you can expect from a contract at a very early stage in discussions.** This will help you to have a realistic view of the likely terms you will be offered and will avoid disappointments that can arise from unrealistic expectations.

3   **Discuss contractual issues early with any co-authors.** Make sure you are each clear about length, scope and completion dates for your manuscript even before you submit your proposal. Make sure they are realistic, allowing for inevitable delays and the difficulties of being jointly responsible for a book.

4   **Clarify your joint position in advance.** Negotiate who will be the principal contact with the commissioning editor, who will be the first named author and how the royalties will be split (publishers will generally assume equally unless you inform them otherwise). If either of you feels strongly about keeping one or more subsidiary rights, you should make a joint decision on this before you negotiate with your editor.

5   **Read through your whole contract point by point when it comes through.** You must read every word and check you understand the implications, even though it may comprise ten or twelve pages of close text. Time spent at this stage can save anguish later.

6   **Make sure you understand all the implications of the clauses.** It is amazing how often authors fail, for example, to notice that they are responsible themselves for producing an index and are horrified to learn that if they do not do so, they can be charged by the publisher to get someone else to do it, even though this has quite clearly been specified in the contract.

7   **Be clear about what rights you are giving up to your publisher.** These may include rights for foreign language sales, for publication in electronic formats, for serials and films, for supplements, revisions and sometimes even future editions. Similarly most contracts will give the publisher 'world rights' that is, the right to sell it or license its sale in all countries. If you want to retain any of these rights, the only opportunity to do so is before the contract is signed.

8   **Make sure you understand who retains the copyright in your work.** It doesn't automatically stay with the author, although these days it is normally possible for an author to retain it, so long as this is confirmed at the contract stage. Don't let your natural delight at being offered a contract lead you to sign up to anything with which you are not happy.

9   **Understand exactly what the contract makes you responsible for.** Although often not expressed in the plainest of language, the contract should nevertheless be very clear about your responsibilities. For example, you need to be clear whether it is you or your publisher who is responsible for obtaining (and indeed paying for) any permissions (and fees) required for the use of extracts, figures or photographs to be used from previously published sources.

10 **Check whether you are signing yourself up to produce 'camera-ready' quality artwork.** If so, then you are responsible for providing all diagrams, charts, images and photographs in a form that can immediately be inserted into the text. Be sure you are capable of doing so before you agree to do it.

11 **Clarify who has responsibility to check the accuracy of the material.** This is particularly important in any areas where material could be regarded as libellous or defamatory.

12   **Don't be afraid to go back and check anything you don't understand.** Particularly if this is your first contract, ask your commissioning editor to clarify matters if there is anything you don't understand. Don't just sign and hope for the best.

13   **Ask about the royalties.** Find out whether these will be paid on net receipts or cover price. Find out how often and when you will be paid and when you will receive royalty statements. (This is particularly important so that you can keep your tax affairs in good order).

14   **Ask advice on contracts from friends and colleagues who have had books published.** Such people can run an eye over your contract and give advice on whether what you are being offered seems reasonable enough. They may be able to advise you on amendments you might suggest to the contract to maximize your royalties or to retain more rights. Don't expect them to be legal experts, however, and trust to your own judgement as well. If in doubt, ask a lawyer to check a contract through with you (although this may eat up most of your royalties in fees).

15   **Don't be afraid to negotiate terms with your editor.** Don't be so overawed by the whole process that you feel too intimidated to propose amendments. Clearly the point at which any publisher might agree to changes will depend on how important the book is to them, but there is no harm in tactfully approaching them on matters such as royalties, advances and the split of fees on certain subsidiary clauses, for example, as serial rights.

16   **Clarify early with your publisher if you wish to retain any rights.** For niche publishing, publishers will make their financial calculations on the basis of world rights and all subsidiary rights and may well rely on estimated revenue from subsidiary rights sales when making you an offer.

17   **Tell your publisher early if you want to go it alone in some areas.** If you have your own publishing contacts in the US, for example, or Australasia, and wish to offer only UK and European rights, this could make your publisher decide against the viability of taking on your book. However, they may have little expectation of doing anything in certain geographical areas and may be happy to leave you to negotiate those separately.

18   **Keep your signed contract in a safe place.** It is an important legal document that you may wish to refer to in detail at some point in the future.

32

Money matters

Don't expect your book royalties to change your lifestyle. Unless you're writing a fiction best-seller, you are unlikely to notice any real difference to your financial state when your royalty cheques arrive. However, getting yourself published may well have different financial rewards, helping towards promotion, getting a new job entirely, or being invited to travel to interesting places to talk about what you've written. The following suggestions, however, are about minding your pennies, so that the financial side of your publishing work goes as well as you can manage it.

1   **Be aware of the normal range of royalty rates.** Such rates vary considerably, depending upon the sort of work being published. Academic rates often start at 5 per cent, while most fiction starts at 10 per cent. The most popular *starting* rates are 7.5 per cent for a paperback book, and 10 per cent for a hardback book, but when your fame grows you will have some opportunity to negotiate with your publisher.

2   **Consider asking for an escalating royalty rate.** Many publishers will agree to include an escalating rate in your contract if you ask. This means that the rate increases when sales reach certain targets. For example, a specialist academic monograph might initially have a planned print run of 1500 copies. If sales reach 2000 copies, royalties may be agreed to increase from 7.5 per cent to 10 per cent, and if sales exceed 5000 copies, up again to 12.5 per cent.

3   **Remember that royalties are related directly to sales.** Royalties are not a mysterious reward system that authors can hope to enjoy irrespective of how well books sell. They are paid out as a fixed percentage of the revenue generated by each copy of your book that is actually purchased.

4   **Make sure you know what your royalty rate will be based on.** A few contracts offer to pay royalties based on the publisher's book cover price. However, the vast majority of royalties are now paid on 'net receipts'.

5 **Know what 'net receipt' means.** Such royalties mean that you will receive 7.5 per cent (or whatever) of the amount received by your publisher for the book. This varies depending upon the discounts which your publisher may offer to chains and bookshops, international agents and co-publishers, all of which are separately negotiated by your publisher. The minimum book trade discount is often of the order of 35 per cent off the cover price (and this means correspondingly less royalties for you).

6 **Ask for a royalty advance, if you need one.** Most publishers will offer a modest advance payment to be deducted later from royalties. This is a token of their commitment to publishing a book. If such an advance is not offered initially, it is worth asking for one. £200 is not uncommon in the UK for an advance, and such a sum can be of help regarding the expenses you will incur as you press on with your writing. Royalty advances may be made in stages. They are often agreed to be paid in two or three stages, for example, the first on signature of the contract, the second on acceptance of your manuscript by the publisher. (Note that this is not the same as on delivery of what may turn out to be a first draft manuscript.) The third stage would normally be on the date of publication of your book. Remember that the official publication date will generally be set for six or so weeks after the printed copies are delivered to the publisher.

7 **Remember that royalty *advances* are just that!** If you do get a royalty advance, don't be disappointed if your first royalty statement shows a negative balance. It will take a varying amount of time for the sales of your book to cover the amount of the advance paid out. It will all depend upon how quickly, and in what volume, your book sells.

8 **Note that royalties are split among co-authors.** If you are co-writing a book, you will need to agree how the royalties will be shared, 50 : 50, 60 : 40 or some other way. Make sure that your publisher knows what you intend, so that a final clause can be added to your contracts confirming the split, and formalizing each author's agreement to this. Remember that the total rates shown in your contract will be divided up as you agree in this clause.

9 **Know your subsidiary rights.** Royalties may also be earned from such arrangements. Many of the clauses in your contract will relate to each and every format your work could ever be produced in, such as on cassette, on a software disk, as a serial extract in a newspaper, and so on. If, for example, a journal or edited volume may in the future reproduce a chapter from your book, you could receive the agreed percentage of the fee negotiated in your contract. Usually, subsidiary clauses split such fees 50 : 50 with your publisher. Such arrangements can bring in unexpected additional royalty payments.

10   **Note the timescales.** All monies are usually paid either annually or six-monthly. Most publishing companies operate a complex computerized royalty accounting system. This will usually calculate all earnings on a set basis. If your book is published one month before the end of your publisher's accounting period, you will get a statement showing one month's sales.

11   **Get to know the format of your royalty statements.** If there's anything in your first statement that you do not understand, ring your editor or the royalties manager and ask for it to be explained. A range of abbreviations can be used, and sales may be grouped into different clusters such as 'high discount', 'low discount', 'gratis', 'bulk', and the way book sales are divided into these types can seem a little strange to authors at first.

12   **Check your royalty statement.** Publishers have occasionally confessed to making errors in their statements, generally blamed on their computers. It is worth checking that the correct royalty rates are shown in calculations. Query anything that seems strange to you.

13   **Have a rough idea of the total amount of money that you may earn on your book.** At contract stage, your publisher will already have provisionally set the cover price for your book, and the likely initial print run. A rough rule of thumb would be to multiply 85 per cent of the initial print run by 65 per cent of the cover price by the agreed royalty percentage to reach an estimate of your total anticipated earnings. If the publisher plans to print 3000 copies and sell them at £10 and your royalty rate is 7.5 per cent, then you would expect to earn about £1243 in total.

14   **Understand your publisher's mark-up principle.** As a rule of thumb, your publisher will budget at proposal stage for the total production costs that will be involved in producing x copies of your book. This figure will then usually be multiplied by six or seven to arrive at the recommended cover price. Any unforeseen increase in the production process will have a knock-on effect in increasing the end price, within a range deemed acceptable in the market place. The mark-up is to take account of the publisher's overheads, the likely 40 per cent discount for bookshops, the author royalties and a marketing contribution for the publisher.

15   **Check in advance whether your publisher will meet any kind of expenses.** While publishers generally don't pay travelling or other expenses for authors, it might be that you could get your publisher to agree to cover your expenses to participate in an author-signing event to launch your book.

16   **Remember to budget for any permission fees which might be involved.**
      If you are using diagrams or extracts from other published works (with
      permission, of course), some fee will generally have been set. In most
      cases your contract will state that these are the author's responsibility.

17   **Check what discount you will be given by your publisher.** Usually your
      publisher will grant you a generous discount if you want to purchase any
      books from their lists. This might be around one third off the published
      price. Any books so purchased may be offset against royalties, if they are
      anticipated in the next few months, with your editor's approval. If you
      need bulk quantities of your own book, for example 150 or more, you
      might be able to negotiate a higher discount rate.

18   **Find out if any grant funds are available to support publication of your
      work.** Don't forget to apply for any university bursaries, research grants
      and so on that your proposed publication might be eligible for.

19   **Keep good records of your royalty income, and your expenses.** Sooner
      or later you'll have to account for your earnings for tax purposes. It can
      be very useful to have clear receipts for anything that is clearly deductible
      from your earnings, such as necessary expenses directly connected with
      the preparation of your book.

Chapter 4   Writing for journals

33   Targeting the right journal
34   Making your research publishable
35   Using the literature search effectively
36   Finding the right voice
37   Style points
38   Improving your 'hit rate'
39   Responding to referees' feedback
40   Dealing with rejections

Authors have many different reasons for wishing to get their work published in reputable journals. For many, it is the way to respect in their fields of research, and to increased funding for their future. For some, the way leads to promotion or to a better post in another organization or institution. The waters are very crowded in the area of publication in the best journals, however, and this chapter aims to point you in the right direction to strike out firmly towards your target.

'Targeting the right journal' is not as easy as you may think. Even the most famous authors in your field may have started by getting their work published in much less prestigious journals than you now see from their current publications. Getting your research published depends rather a lot on whether it is publishable. This in turn depends on the words you use to put it across. Our next five sets of suggestions address this matter from different points of view, starting with making it clear to yourself exactly *what* you're really trying to communicate, and to whom. 'Using the literature search effectively' is important, as the quality of your own work will be judged partly on how well you sum up and analyse what has been published already in your field. 'Finding the right voice' and 'Style points' offer suggestions about how you can start finding the best way for you to make your presence felt in the publications in your field. 'Improving your hit rate' rounds off our suggestions about how to maximize your own chance of getting your work published in reputable journals.

But what if it all goes wrong? That's what it sometimes feels like when we get referees' comments on our work, and find out only too quickly that what we thought was a watertight paper or article is in fact riddled with holes. However, that is often just the starting point from which will develop a much *better* publication than the one that was originally submitted. Our suggestions about 'Responding to referees' feedback' are hard-won from experience!

Our final set of suggestions in this chapter is about 'Dealing with rejections'. This is not an easy thing to do, at least until one realizes that all of the distinguished and well-known authorities in any field have learned to do this too, and *still* experience rejections from time to time themselves.

33

Targeting the right journal

Editors reject papers mostly because they are not suited to the journal. As many as half of all papers submitted to a journal never enter the review process. The journal may be fundamentally theoretical, yet an author submits a paper based on practice – or, vice versa. The journal may be overtly international in scope, yet a proposed paper pays no attention to anything outside the home country. The following suggestions will help you target the right journal.

1 **Broaden your scope.** Everyone in their respective fields wants to get published in the most highly-rated journal. That's why those journals have rejection rates in the high nineties. Inexperienced authors may break through immediately, but it's unlikely. Commit to widening your prospects from the one or two most famous journals to the ten which are highly respectable.

2 **Ask respected colleagues.** You'll find out more about publishing possibilities by talking with those who are already widely published. Talk to them – to your supervisor, department head, counterparts in other institutions. Find out where they first became published and what journals they read apart from the most obvious.

3 **Conduct a citation search.** Trace the publication records of those authors whom you respect. You may have read them most recently in the top journal, but where did they publish five or ten years ago?

4 **Check directories.** Every university library will have at least one major directory listing journals, their editors, their objectives and their addresses. You will be surprised at the number of possibilities which exist in your field.

5 **Study copies of your prospective journals.** Again, this may seem obvious, yet many editors report that papers they receive have been written without regard to the journal's objectives and style. If your own library doesn't have the journals you want to review, source them by inter-library loan or ask the publisher to send you samples. Many paper-based journals now have web-sites with editorial direction and selected articles.

6 **Study key issues of each journal.** Journal editors and advisors often comment importantly on the direction of their journals at strategic times of the year. In the last issue of the journal, editors will often summarize the high points of the year and describe what they found to be the most useful or insightful papers. In the first issue of a new year or volume, the editor may describe the kinds of papers being sought in the future.

7 **Obtain Notes for Authors.** The editorial team has painstakingly devised clear instructions for authors to follow. Their advisory notes detail everything from the editorial objectives to the preferred style of referencing. These are usually found in each issue of the journal, or at least in the first of each volume.

8 **Get into the minds of your audience.** Who exactly is the editor and what does he or she like? Read the editorials and anything the editor has written recently. Editors are not in the business of keeping secrets from prospective authors. Seek to understand what excites, annoys and bores the editor.

9 **Trace the evolution of thinking.** Many authors publish frequently in the same journal and refer to their earlier work and the work of fellow authors. How will your work fit in? Can you see how you can contribute to a particular's journal's progress in becoming or maintaining a leading edge position?

10 **Solicit early advice.** While most journal editors say they prefer to receive a manuscript rather than a query, few can resist a carefully targeted letter designed to assess their interest. Something like, 'Your encouraging comment in No 1 Vol 8 about the value of a multi-disciplinary approach prompted me to send you the attached abstract of my forthcoming paper', will often capture an editor's attention.

34

Making your research publishable

What is your paper about? Why should anyone read it? You may think the answers to those questions are implicit in your work, and you may be right. But if you don't make them explicit, your paper will never be published in a respectable journal. In this chapter we will explore the key variables which make your research publishable.

1   **What is the purpose of your paper?** Many papers are rejected simply because the editor and review board can't figure out what they're supposed to be saying. We suspect that's because the research is still seen by the author as an end in itself. Now is the time to consider the outcome rather than the process.

2   **Write it in 20 words or less.** Draw yourself out of the role of researcher into the role of communicator. Take your years of effort and summarize all of it in 20 words or less. 'The purpose of this paper is to…' Demonstrate a new technique? Refute an old theory? Answer a puzzling question?

3   **Don't lose your nerve.** The reason many papers lack a clearly stated purpose is not so much because the author doesn't know what it is, but because the author doesn't want to say it so boldly. It can be a salutary moment: 'Am I really going to nail my ideas down and tell the world exactly what I've done and why they should listen?'

4   **Purpose leads to practice.** Once you are clear and confident about your purpose, review your research to develop its real implications. These could be for immediate application or for further research – but sometime soon you will have to say – 'so what?'

5   **Write why it matters.** Our research into acceptance criteria revealed that, all other criteria being met, the most common reason for rejection was that the implications of the paper were not clear. 'So what?' reviewers would ask. Take your research and write two clear sentences (20 words or less) explaining exactly why your research is important and what the reader should do about it.

6   **Define your scope.** A barrier to focus sometimes arises when we fear that readers will challenge us on why we centred on some aspects of our research and not on others. You may by now have taken your scope for granted. Try to summarize it in one short paragraph to help clarify your thinking.

7   **Articulate its limitations.** Time, money, resources, challenges of data gathering – all of these have imposed constraints upon your research. Again, we sometimes fear that others will challenge us about these. Now is the time to review and summarize the limitations that affected your work.

8   **Accept your imperfections.** As one doctoral supervisor notably said: 'There are only two types of articles; those that are perfect and never get published, and those that are good enough and do'. There will always be another question, always another, better way to have approached your research. Recognize that and carry on. Accepting your imperfections isn't called failure, it's called learning.

9   **Draft your structure.** This will not define your final treatment, but now that you know what you are saying and why, review your research under the following headings: purpose, implications, methodology, analysis, conclusion.

10   **Give it a rest.** The above process is lengthy and time-consuming, but it will quite probably be the determining factor in whether or not your paper ever gets written, let alone published. Allow the effort to settle down and resist the temptation to think it's an end in itself. Next, you will take your draft structure and begin to relate it to the needs of different groups of readers.

35

Using the literature search effectively

Few sections of a research paper are more enervating than a mundane literature review. That's because many researchers don't so much review the literature as they summarize and faithfully report on it. It's time to go well beyond an undergraduate description of who said what when, and on to an analytical exposition of who said what when and why it was important (or not) and what you think should be done about it.

1   **Plan to reveal, not just review.** You have amassed hundreds of papers and read scores of books. All of your reading impacted on your research – but not all of it is directly relevant to a single paper about your research. Decide at the outset that you will use only what is necessary to inform your reader.

2   **We've seen it all before.** Remember, the editor and review board knows the broad field better than you do. They won't be impressed by three pages of irrelevant references, all of which could have simply been lifted from another book or database.

3   **Review your scope.** The effort you spent describing your scope will be of real benefit here. The literature you describe and analyse will be that which reflects your chosen scope, not necessarily all aspects of the field.

4   **Review your beginning and end.** The literature needs to follow the purpose and support or be refuted by your implications. Now that you have articulated your purpose and implications, selecting the emphasis for your literature section will follow naturally.

5   **Summarize the relevant literature.** As a first step, draw together the key contributors who impact on your field and, in particular, on your specific research and its scope. Of all whom you have read, you will want to describe most fully the work of those with the most impact on your implications.

6   **Synthesize the work of key contributors.** Summarizing the relevant literature is where many people stop, but you need to go further. This is where you will make sense of your predecessors' work. You can synthesize along chronological lines, showing how your understanding has arisen systematically from one person's idea to the next, or according to key themes or questions.

7   **Analyse the work so far.** Now that you have summarized and made sense of your predecessors, here's your opportunity to comment upon it, revealing their strengths and weaknesses, brilliance and failings. This is a most useful and interesting part of any literature and shows your ability to evaluate critically the work of others.

8   **Put your stamp on it – authorize.** This is where authors make the vital connection between what the body of knowledge has offered so far, and what their contribution now is. This is where you ask the burning question foremost in your reviewers' minds: 'so what'? How is your research going to support or challenge the existing thinking? What will other people learn from what you've done?

9   **Edit without mercy.** Having done all of the above, your literature review will still be too long and unwieldy. It's terribly difficult to resist the opportunity to show off our erudition, and name-dropping is the most convenient way to do it. Go back over your review and cut away all but what is essential, forcing yourself to be concise, analytical and conclusive.

10   **Don't over refer to your own publications.** Too many references to your own work (however relevant you feel it may be) can make you seem boastful. It is easy to be tempted to include all of your own references whether they are relevant or not, especially as you are likely to have accurate details to hand.

36

Finding the right voice

How we hear an author speak is known as a 'voice'. Authors speak through writing, of course, not the spoken word, but the tone of voice in an article can be as clear as if we were hearing human speech. Just as we interpret someone's meaning partly through their tone of voice when they speak, so we interpret meaning through the voice of the written word. Here we present some suggestions about finding and articulating the right voice.

1   **Read, read, read.** Have you ever wondered why you sometimes know that a sentence doesn't 'sound right' – or that it does? Your mind and inner hearing are attuned to certain rhythms and resonances embedded in grammatical convention. You nurtured that sense through reading. Read selected journals regularly and you will begin to condition yourself to their tone.

2   **Any voice might do.** There isn't an absolute right or wrong about voice. Some journals like articles which begin with snappy sentences in journalistic style, while others prefer a more formal academic tone. Find out what your selected journals want by studying their editorial guidelines and reading them regularly.

3   **Prefer the positive to the negative.** A pompous tone evolves as we use certain structures. One of the most obvious is expressing something in a negative tone. 'This research is not unlike that which…' is a negative expression of 'This research is similar to…'.

4   **Prefer the active to the passive.** Even academic formal writing is brightened by reducing the number of passive sentences. Rather than saying 'authors have frequently been troubled by rejection', try 'rejection frequently troubles authors'. Check your wordprocessing package for the grammar check function and use it to highlight your passive sentences.

5   **Seek to express, not impress.** Using long, obscure words shrouds your writing with an aura of mystery which you may mistake for erudition. It is neither clever nor interesting to force your reader to check a dictionary every few paragraphs, and only increases your tone of pomposity.

6   **Invite your reader into your world.** Dispensing with jargon altogether will improve the inviting tone of your voice. The more often your reader must pause to work out what you mean by a curious phrase or abbreviation (and shame on the editor who lets these pass), the less inviting your voice sounds.

7   **Vary your sentence length.** Long sentences are more difficult to follow, even if they are grammatically pristine. Now and then they can be useful and even engaging, but strung together they add a sombre note to your work which makes your voice sound heavy. Intersperse them with short sentences to vary the pace and brighten the tone.

8   **Eliminate personal asides.** The tone of most academic journals is formal, to greater or lesser degrees, but strikingly different from a short magazine piece. One of the distinctions is that of familiarity. Academic researchers should be distancing themselves from the reader sufficiently to allow a more objective review of the work.

9   **Pass your paper around.** This is one occasion where no previous experience is necessary. Ask your friends, family, colleagues and acquaintances to read portions of your writing and tell you how they hear your voice. Amend where you must until it matches the voice of the journal you aspire to. (Oh, yes, not ending a sentence with a preposition is a rule made to be broken if it matches your voice!)

10 **Develop your own range of voices.** The more you write, the more comfortable you are likely to be writing in different voices for different audiences. Aim to write as naturally as you can in whatever voice you've chosen for each particular purpose, and you will soon develop the knack of making your work come across well to quite different audiences.

37

Style points

Style is that sometimes indefinable quality which gives a certain personality or character to someone or something. But style doesn't happen by accident. Components of style are often not unique; a black hat and a pair of black gloves will not alone create a stylish outfit, but the combination will. Creating personal style requires paying attention to the components of your writing and the way you put them all together. We review here some common characteristics of stylish writing.

1   **Whose style is it?** Every publication has its own 'housestyle' to govern such variations as headings, footnotes, reference systems and so on. These are the mechanics which will help make your paper easy for the publisher to process. Whatever variations on the themes of style you may choose, housestyle is not an option.

2   **Take care of the basics.** Papers which are ugly to look at and hard to read may not receive the attention they deserve. Your adherence to points of commonly accepted style plus the journal's housestyle demonstrates that you have a good grasp of the language. Make sure you get these right before attempting to impose your own personal idiosyncrasies.

3   **Economy is the best value.** Always err on the side of brevity. If you can't summarize your research and implications in a few short sentences, you may not have the clear focus so necessary for clear writing. Once you start writing, continue to edit and shorten rather than expand and lengthen.

4   **Throw away your thesaurus.** A short word is always better than a longer substitute. Most of the time we know the right word but try to find a longer one because we think it's more impressive. It's not. What impresses reviewers and readers is your ability to communicate simply and clearly.

5   **Double-check for meaning.** It's sometimes surprising how often academics will choose the wrong words to express an idea – confusing their infers and implies, illusions and allusions, effects and affects. The number one rule of writing figures here: when in doubt, check it out. Don't let the bad habits you may have developed take over when a quick glance at a dictionary would set you right.

6   **Check spelling.** No points here for trying to position yourself as a world-leading academic when you haven't bothered to check your spelling. No one is a perfect speller, which is why software includes the spell-check function. Of course, it's not infallible and won't correct your its and theirs, but activating it should be an automatic gesture before saving any file.

7   **Punctuation should enhance understanding.** The reason we have commas, full stops (periods), semi-colons and parentheses is because they help the reader grasp our meaning. If you don't know the difference between a colon and semi-colon, either find out or don't use them. The punctuation check deserves the time of an experienced copy-editor.

8   **Metaphors are a slippery slope to hoe.** Most of the time, we use metaphors because we can't be bothered to say what we really mean. We choose, instead, to allude to a picture. Pictures can be vibrant, but most aren't. Most metaphors are so hackneyed that the reader glosses over them without gaining anything new. Think carefully before using metaphors, and when you do, make sure you don't mix them up.

9   **Ask other people specifically about your style.** This is actually rather harder to do than to ask people for feedback on your content, as style is somewhat more personal, and you may find it harder to view critical comments objectively. Check your style out with a friend. A second opinion often helps you to see your work anew.

10 **Work on it.** Writing is a craft, and like any craft it needs to be mastered through understanding and practice. Your library and bookshop have shelves of books devoted to the finer points of style. Now that you've decided to be a writer as well as an academic, you should take the time to develop the skill just as you took the time to develop your knowledge of your speciality.

38

Improving your 'hit rate'

The previous sections in this chapter have outlined the most important steps to help you achieve your publishing goals. If you take them slowly, step-by-step, you will greatly improve your chances of becoming published. Here's our summary of how you will get there.

1   **Clear your mind before you clear your desk.** Don't distract yourself with the thousand seemingly important tasks – like organizing your paper clips or buying new pencils – that will blur your focus. Start by concentrating on summarizing the value of your research until you can say it in a simple sentence in your sleep.

2   **Decide who will be interested.** Your research now is sharply focused. That being so, you will limit your potential audience. That improves your chances of becoming published. Make a list of the two or three target groups with whom you want to communicate.

3   **Confer with trusted colleagues.** Take the time now to share your focus and ideas about your audience with others in your field. Solicit and accept their constructive feedback. The more often you open your work to those who represent your particular reference group, the more likely it is they will help you refine your approach.

4   **Choose your potential journals carefully.** Properly focused research and its eventual publication will only interest a handful of journals. Read them, understand them, and make sure you have their notes of guidance to potential authors. Most papers are rejected simply because they do not match the editorial objectives of the journal.

5   **Quality is what the customer says it is.** The quality of your research and paper is judged by those who intend to benefit by it. They are the ones – the editors, reviewers and readers – who will determine the quality criteria upon which your paper is assessed. Find out what those criteria are.

6   **Make it interesting.** Most published papers are never read in their entirety. This is partly because the research findings need only be glanced at to determine their value for the reader, but it's also because many academic papers are tedious and boring. Improve your hit rate by making your work vivid and exciting.

7   **Make sure you know why it matters.** Another common reason for rejection is the 'so what?' clause. Reviewers often can't figure out why your paper is supposedly important – mainly because you're not telling them! Draw out implications throughout – of your research question, of your methodology, of the literature, of your findings.

8   **Make it readable.** Turgid, vague, verbose papers are no fun to read. The reviewer may be forced through professional duty to read it, but if it's a struggle then the likelihood is it will be rejected or returned for revision.

9   **Follow your instructions.** If an editor or reviewer makes a condition or even a strong suggestion, follow it. These are the people who exist to help you transform your research into a masterful piece of fascinating prose. Work with them, not against them.

10   **Remain above reproach.** By adhering to housestyle guidelines, reviewers' comments and deadlines you will make everyone's life easier. People prefer to work with those who make their lives easier, not more difficult.

11   **Only submit to one journal at a time.** Editors' schedules are ruined by authors who submit to more than one journal. Journals want to have original, new material. Although this means you must wait until you hear from each editor in turn, it certainly prevents you from being blacklisted by weary editors.

12   **And just keep doing it!** The more you write, the better a writer you become. The more often you submit papers, the more likely you are to be accepted. The more often your papers are accepted, the more likely it is future papers will be accepted. And so on!

39

Responding to referees' feedback

Let's say you have reached the stage in the publication process when you receive feedback from the review panel. What do you do? When do you do it? How do you do it? We wouldn't be posing these questions unless we assumed that many authors don't manage this stage well. And they don't. Some ignore the feedback entirely, while others respond in a way which endears them to the reviewers' and the editor. Let's see how they do it.

1   **Choose to respond.** There are two black holes in the publishing process. This is when the editor feels he or she has lost control and is at the mercy of outside forces. The first occurs when a reviewer doesn't send back comments in time, and the second occurs when the author doesn't respond. Decide now that if you are entering the process you will honour the implicit assumption of participation.

2   **Acknowledge the editor.** Comments are normally sent to an author via the editor or the editorial staff. You are invited to consider the reviewers' remarks and make the suggested alterations, usually by a given date. Immediately, acknowledge that you have received the letter and will be complying by the deadline. This makes it possible for your paper to be tentatively scheduled in a future issue.

3   **Accept the feedback with good grace.** As you have by now committed to the process, part of the deal is that you will accept that peer review is the benchmark by which you will be judged. Given that you have, we hope, targeted the journal carefully, you should now assume that the review panel has made the correct judgement. Some of their comments may grate a little, but such is the pain that comes with learning.

4   **Confer with colleagues.** The reviewers' feedback may only amount to a few paragraphs or sentences. While most reviewers take time to ensure that their meaning is clear, it is wise at this stage to ask other people to help you interpret the suggestions. Your co-author's supervisor and other close associates should be sent copies of the comments and asked to discuss them with you.

5   **Re-read the journal.** Remember that the people reviewing your paper are busy reviewing other papers for the same journal. If the reviewer seems particularly interested in certain aspects, say, your description of your instruments or your lack of guidance for further researchers, read other articles which attend to those points. This will help you deepen your understanding of what the reviewer is exploring.

6   **What if you can't?** Perhaps a review comment concerns you because it attacks something you feel reveals a basic flaw in your original research or its design. You can't go back and do that piece all over again, although in the future you might decide to do it differently. We recommend that you don't arrive at any conclusion before discussing the comments with respected colleagues. It might be that the reviewer is asking for more explanation rather than suggesting your method or design was wrong.

7   **What if you still can't?** If you finally conclude that the reviewer has illuminated something which can't be fixed, admit it. Don't ignore it or try to write something other than what you've been asked to do. You might instead choose to suggest to the editor that the paper be revised taking that very problem as its starting point: 'How not to do research by this method' and might therefore contribute to the work of other researchers about to make the same mistake.

8   **Revise as requested.** All being well, you will be able to make the amendments according to the suggestions and the deadline. Keep in mind that when you submit your revised paper, your amendments will be checked against the reviewers' original comments. This is no time for lip service.

9   **Return your paper on time.** Whatever other commitments you have at the moment, this one takes priority. The editor and reviewers have all invested their time and wisdom in your paper – don't insult them now by saying you have something better to do.

10 **Say 'thank you'.** It won't ensure that your paper is published, but it will reinforce in your own mind and heart that this is one of the best exercises in receiving free advice and support that you've ever been given.

40

Dealing with rejections

Even for well published authors, there is a feeling of suspense when opening that letter from a publisher or editor which contains the verdict on a piece of your work. When this letter (or fax or phone call) is a bringer of bad news, the following suggestions may provide both comfort and support.

1   **Don't be surprised.** Whether it was a book proposal or an article submitted to a journal, there are many more letters of rejection written to authors than letters of unconditional acceptance. If you get a rejection, remind yourself that you're now in really distinguished company. We know of no significant author who has not had such letters.

2   **Don't be surprised even if you're a well-published author.** If your writing is already respected, it can come as a bit of a shock if your latest piece is being rejected. However, there can be many sensible reasons for rejecting it, including that it may not be the most wonderful piece that you've ever written!

3   **Watch out for your ego.** It's all too easy to become defensive, and to become hostile to the people who have dared not to accept your masterpiece. Resist the temptation to put pen to paper to defend the validity and importance of your work. It's worth putting the piece and letter away for a week or more, and returning to it later when emotions have subsided.

4   **If rejection hurts, question your motives.** Are you more interested in being vindicated than in getting your work published? It helps to regard getting your work accepted as a game with many variables, where you're constantly trying to make adjustments to your strategy on the basis of experience, and where there is still a considerable element of chance involved.

5   **Don't stop writing.** When one piece of your work has been rejected by one target publisher or journal, this does not mean that all of your work will be rejected by the whole world. It can be very healthy to redirect your energies, for a while at least, into something else that you're already working on.

6   **Check out whether your piece has really been rejected.** Some rejections are definite and without any statement of reasons or suggestions. However, many rejections are accompanied by explanations, which could be very useful to you in your next piece of writing. Furthermore, rejections are often conditional, and give suggestions regarding ways you could recompose your writing to make it more acceptable to the targeted publisher or journal.

7   **If it's just a matter of 'length', change it.** Publishers and editors normally work to tight page limits, particularly regarding journal articles or book chapters. If your submission is too long, swallow that pride and get cutting. Decide which are the most important parts of the ideas you wish to communicate, and prune out some of the rest. Most articles are all the better for being two-thirds of the original length!

8   **Remember that there are many good reasons for rejecting a good article or proposal.** If your publisher just does not want another book in an area that is well represented in their catalogue, or if your article is just not tuned in to the needs and interests of the readership of a particular journal, it does not mean that there's anything wrong with your writing. One of the factors leading to successful publication is getting the material to the right place at the right time, and there is no shame in not managing to do this very often.

9   **If your referees or reviewers have made suggestions, take heed of them.** It takes no longer to follow up most of these suggestions than it would to write an eloquent exposition regarding how the suggestions are not at all appropriate in the context of your work. Even if you find yourself including discussions that you would rather not have brought into your work, the fact that you have had such topics suggested to you indicates that some readers at least will wish to see such discussions.

10 **If you're going to make changes and have another go, move fast.** Publishers and editors have tight windows, and if you miss your time slot they will not be able to consider your work further. In any case, it often takes no longer to get started on the business of making some changes, than to sit putting off the actual moment of starting.

11 **If there's nothing you can do with your rejected piece, don't throw it away in disgust.** You may never be able to publish it in the form which it is in at present, but future circumstances may turn it into a good starting point from which to write something else. Also, it's worth keeping your mistakes to remind you not to make the same ones again.

12 **Rejection of your writing is not rejection of you as a worthwhile person.** Be bold and talk about the rejection, positively, with your friends. They will still be friends.

Chapter 5   Getting it right

41   Introductions, forewords and prefaces
42   Getting the language right
43   Getting feedback on drafts
44   Manuscript appeal
45   Diagrams, drawings and tables
46   Making a good finish
47   Getting the references right
48   Writing a glossary
49   Compiling an index
50   Checking proofs
51   Copyright and rights
52   What *is* publication?

This chapter covers a lot of ground. In particular, many sections here address the minutiae which make up a good publication, whether it is an article, paper or book.

There is no second chance to make a good first impression on your readers (and editors and reviewers). This is why we start with suggestions about 'Introductions, forewords and prefaces'. Also, 'Getting the language right' for your target audience is crucial, and the best way of working towards the right language is to use all of the feedback that you can get on draft versions of your work. This leads us into 'Manuscript appeal', and a look at the things that editors and reviewers like (and hate) most.

If your work involves the use of drawings, diagrams, tables, photographs and so on, it is particularly important to ensure that they appear in your final published work exactly as you would wish them to, and also that getting them to this state does not take you (or your publisher) an inordinate amount of time and energy. We hope that our suggestions about this will help both to save you time, and to make your illustrations serve you well.

Our next section is entitled 'Making a good finish'. A paper, article, or even chapter that just 'fizzles out' will have nothing like the impact of a well rounded off piece of writing. However, coming to a robust conclusion is not the end of your work when writing an article or even book. There are the references to check up on. Reviewers and copy-editors have eagle-eyes when it comes to references, and will soon spot missing dates, missing places of publication, and even wrong volume numbers.

'Writing a glossary' and 'Compiling an index' when you have written or co-written a book, are quite straightforward tasks, but can be quite daunting if it is the first time you have tackled them. Both of these tasks are usefully done at proof stage, providing that is, that you have agreed in advance with your publisher that you will do this. We also offer some suggestions on the vital business of 'Checking proofs'. It is best to do this particularly carefully, or else you may end up having to live with mistakes and errors published under your name!

We next give some advice on the matter of 'Copyright and rights'. For new authors this can seem a minefield, and we trust that our suggestions give an insight into the main principles involved in these areas.

We end this chapter with a section entitled 'What *is* publication?' which may contain one or two things that could surprise you!

41

Introductions, forewords and prefaces

A problem with the first pages of many books is that people tend not to read them. If the piece that starts your book is really important, try to make sure people will actually read it. The following suggestions may help you decide how you want your book to begin.

1 **Write the introduction last.** It's only when you've written the whole of your book, paper, or chapter, that you really know what is in it, and how best to introduce it. It is of course useful to have a 'working' version of the introduction available while you write your work, but it is rare for this to turn out to be the ideal starting page(s) for the final version.

2 **Work out what you want to call it.** There are several possibilities, including 'Introduction', 'Foreword', 'Preface', and so on. In publishers' eyes, each of these means something specific. An introduction summarizes the content of your book, a preface sets the scene within a wider context, and a foreword is generally an endorsement of your book written by someone else.

3 **Work out what your first pages are intended to do.** For example, an introductory section may be there to justify why a new book is now needed on the topic. Or it may be there as an important section to link together the various parts of the book, and to explain why things have been arranged in a particular order. Having worked out the purpose, it's often possible to arrive at a useful title for the start of your book, for example: 'Why implement flexible learning?' if the book is intended to help readers start out on such a mission.

4 **Remember that there is no second chance to make a good first impression!** Not everyone will read your first few pages, but for those who do, this is the occasion when they will form important overall

impressions of your book or chapter. It is well worth spending much more time making the beginning read really well. Make it interesting. Don't make it too long. Use several people to gather feedback on whether the first start whets their appetite for what is to follow.

5   **Ensure that the first pages in particular are up to date.** In many areas, events move rapidly, and further important things may have happened between writing your book or chapter and publication date. While it is seldom possible to go through all of your work updating at late stages (even proof stage), it is usually possible to add a significant sentence or two to the first page or two, to show that you know about an important recent development, even though the body of the book does not address it directly.

6   **Decide whether this is the best place for any acknowledgements.** If you need to acknowledge certain people for major help in creating the book as a whole, they probably deserve to go in the opening pages. When acknowledgements are more general, such as for suggestions made during piloting of draft versions, it is probably best to have a separate 'Acknowledgements' section, rather than include these within the introduction.

7   **Invite a big name in your field to write a foreword.** A glowing foreword written by a well-known authority can enhance the sales of your book. Quotations from this can be used to good effect in the publisher's promotional materials. If you have any useful contacts who could write such a foreword, don't be afraid to use them.

8   **Get agreement from your foreword writer at draft manuscript stage.** When the invited authority has agreed in principle to provide a foreword at an early stage, then you can let your publisher know to build in space in advance.

9   **Give a word count and timescale to your foreword writer.** Let the person concerned know that 300 words (or whatever) is what you are looking for, and that it will be needed at proof stage, which is expected to be (say) July. You should arrange for the writer to be sent a set of page proofs of the whole book, with (for example) ten days to deliver the foreword. Don't forget to ensure that the writer will receive a copy of the book, with your thanks, as soon as it is printed. Publishers often allow an additional free copy for such purposes.

10   **If your book has several components at the beginning, order them as follows.** The correct order is foreword, preface then introduction.

42

Getting the language right

Everyone writing for publication needs to take account of the conventions of published prose. Many people have learned traditional rules of punctuation and syntax (but not always too well, as the teaching may not always have been inspired). The suggestions in this section are designed for those who may need to be reminded about some of the conventions, and aims to help prevent you having your copy-edited work sent back to you covered in red ink!

1   **Paragraph your work.** Remember that a paragraph is a unit of thought around which one or more sentences are grouped. There is often a key sentence, usually at the beginning, which carries the burden of the meaning of the paragraph. Other sentences then may exemplify, develop, extend, amplify, or diverge from the original idea. Try to ensure that paragraphs are of a reasonable length, and that the break appears at a logical point in the flow of your text.

2   **Think twice about acronyms, abbreviations and jargon.** Such devices may be effective at communicating ideas succinctly within a relatively closed group of readers. However, anything that makes your writing look as if it's in a foreign language to readers outside your immediate target audience will narrow your readership. It is usually worth deciding whether you really need any shorthand devices, or whether it may be simpler just to spell out terms as and when you need them.

3   **Watch your sentence length.** It's sometimes tempting to use long, complex sentence structures, thinking that this will make your writing more credible. Writing is about effective communication, and it is well established that long sentences increase the chances of important messages failing to get across. Longer sentences with multiple subordinate phrases and clauses can carry more intricate ideas, but may be more difficult for the reader to cope with, especially where the structure of the sentence is complex with multiple elements (as in this example). Choose your places to demonstrate your sophistication with written language, and don't let eloquence conflict with good communication of ideas. Short sentences are often used for emphasis.

4   **Make sure each sentence has an active verb.** Reading sentences that just seem to peter out without going anywhere. Notwithstanding any points you want to get across. Just ends up making your readers infuriated.

5   **Make numbers readable.** Conventions vary, but it is usual to write in words numbers up to ten. It is also a good idea to avoid starting sentences with numbers or percentages. 75 per cent of readers think this looks rather clumsy.

6   **Don't drive your readers dotty with punctuation.** The rules are straightforward, but often broken. Colons precede lists, and do not need a dash after them (: –). Semi-colons are used to separate two short sentences; they can usefully replace a conjunction such as 'and' or 'but'. We often find ourselves telling authors that 'double quotation marks should be reserved for reported speech'. Single quotation marks often indicate words that are 'precieuse' or rare, or used in unfamiliar or special ways. Where the intention is emphasis, **bold** or *italics* are safer alternatives to single quotation marks. One of the authors would argue that parenthetical dashes – arguably wickedly over-used – should never be found in academic writing. (The others disagree.)

7   **Say to yourself 'What I *really* mean is...'.** Then write down your completions of this phrase. If you put yourself into the position of explaining to someone who has just questioned your exact meaning, you often ensure that your meaning will be clear in the first place.

8   **Don't be afraid of short words.** There are always long words which can make your writing appear to be more scholarly. Real scholarship, however, is about ideas and not just words. Well chosen, simple language is usually better at getting important ideas across.

9   **Try listening to your writing.** It can be revealing to get someone to read out a section of your writing, preferably into a tape recorder. Listen to whether someone else's interpretation of tone of voice and emphasis matches that which you yourself would have given if you had read it out aloud. If there are distinct differences, the message could be that your meaning is not yet coming through.

10   **Decide whether contractions are appropriate.** Not everyone likes contractions such as it's, I've, we'll, you've, there's, and so on. Some readers view these as sloppy grammar! However, if your writing is intended to be informal and personal (as in this book), there are distinct advantages in writing in a way that is similar to how you would explain something orally to people.

11 **Watch out for your own pet phrases!** Anything that is repeated too often can be wearing for readers. Ask your pilot readers to look out for these and to tell you about them. Some of our own pet phrases that we've tried to gain control over include 'it is important to…', 'for example when' and 'in other words'. If you find such a phrase coming in too often, use your spellcheck facility to search for instances of it, and replace or omit them as often as you reasonably can.

12 **Make sure your references are spot-on.** Use the referencing convention (eg Harvard) as directed in the 'Notes to Authors' from your publisher. A surprisingly high proportion of copy-editor queries refer to references that don't appear in the text, or references not listed in the bibliography but appearing in the text, or (particularly) to references with missing elements. Make your copy-editor happy by getting them right first time.

13 **Obey spacing conventions.** One convention is to use single spaces after commas, and after full stops (periods). Another is to use two spaces after full stops. If you are using left and right justification on your word-processing package, you may not be able to see which spaces are 'hard' and which ones are inserted by the package. Check whether your author guidelines specify a convention. On word-processing packages it is fairly easy to do a global edit at the end of your writing to (for example) change '. .' to '. '. Remember, however, to save your work immediately before doing any global edit, and to save it as something else immediately after doing such an edit, so you can retrieve things if something serious goes wrong.

43

Getting feedback on drafts

When you're writing something, the most important way to improve it is to get feedback from people. It's not just that authors are the last people to spot their own typographical or grammar errors, though this level of feedback is invaluable in its own right. What you also want is feedback on how the piece of writing serves the purpose for which you are writing it, and that's where your pilot reviewers come in. The following suggestions can help you to make a useful pilot version of your work, and use it to make the final product much better.

1   **Don't wait till it's perfect.** It never will be! It's far better to get your book, article or chapter 80 per cent or so right and then print it out several times, so that you're able to pass drafts on to other people who will give you feedback.

2   **Decide who to ask for feedback.** There are three main things to think about here: punctuality, quality of feedback, and authoritativeness. The best people to ask for feedback are those who've already given you really useful feedback on your past writings! However, if you're starting from scratch, cast your net quite widely, and regard it as research into whom you're going to ask for feedback on your *next* effort. Excellent feedback is no good if it comes too late, and similar comments from more than one person usually means good quality feedback.

3   **Don't just drop it on them!** It's well worth ringing up the people from whom you would like feedback, and asking them if they will be so kind. Promise them something reasonable, such as a copy of your final submission, or even a copy of the finished product if you can afford this. Be wary of people who expect to be paid for the time they may spend giving feedback; they're not usually as good as those who are willing to read your writing out of interest, collegiality or friendship.

4   **Give a firm date by which you want your feedback.** Don't make the timescale too long. If you give people months, they will put it on the shelf for later, and probably forget about it. Make your firm date about two

weeks before you *really* want to start adjusting your material using all the feedback you receive.

5 **Encourage robust feedback.** It's much better to get critical feedback before your work is published, than in adverse reviews. Ask your chosen people direct questions about your draft. These can be along the lines of 'what have I missed out?', 'what have I said too much about?', 'what's the most interesting bit?', 'what's the most opaque bit?', 'who *else* should I have referred to in the references?', and so on.

6 **Check up that your feedback is on its way.** Drop a note, send an e-mail, ring up, anything just to gently remind your pilot reviewers that you're looking forward to receiving their feedback. Sometimes they'll hedge somewhat (having not yet started) then get down quickly to the task having been reminded.

7 **Thank people *immediately*.** As soon as you get your marked-up drafts, pass on your thanks by phone, note or e-mail. It's worth doing this even before you're in a position to weigh up exactly how valuable the feedback turns out to be. When it's really useful, don't hesitate to thank people again, this time explaining what you really appreciate in their feedback, and how you're going to take heed of it.

8 **Don't argue with your pilot reviewers.** Tempting as it is to defend yourself whenever someone criticizes your masterpiece, you don't have to act on every piece of feedback you receive. If only one or two pilot reviewers find a particular fault or weakness, and if everyone else really likes the section concerned, make your own decision about whether it needs adjusting or not. Hold your judgement about what is good feedback and what isn't until you know the whole picture.

9 **Remember to acknowledge the people who give you feedback.** Create your acknowledgements paragraph at the same time as editing your material with their ideas. Don't risk the embarrassment of forgetting who gave you feedback about what, or missing out the name of someone whose feedback was really useful. Thank particular people for particular things as you write your acknowledgements, so that you don't end up thanking the wrong person for a particular idea. Don't forget to acknowledge the people who gave you feedback that you didn't like, or that you decided to ignore; they too have tried to help you.

10 **Remember to keep your promises.** Forward to your pilot reviewers that finished version you said you would send. If you promised free copies of the published product, make sure that you honour your promise. Being good to your pilot reviewers is not just professional, but it also helps these people to be more willing to give you useful feedback on a future occasion.

44

Manuscript appeal

When you're submitting your writing for publication it is well worth trying to make the best of first impressions, particularly those on editors and reviewers. The following suggestions may serve as a checklist.

1   **Make it look professional.** This is easy to ask, and much harder to pin down. Professional looking writing is about the right tone and style for the target audience, and also about avoiding obvious things like misspellings, typographical errors and punctuation anomalies.

2   **Make it look really relevant to the readership of the journal.** This is a key criterion in the minds of journal editors. It is easy for them to reject anything which could be argued to be tangential to the areas covered by the journal, or remote from the interests of the majority of its readers.

3   **Highlight the timeliness of your contribution.** 'Why should this be published *now*?' is a good question to bear in mind when choosing how you introduce your writing. While taking care not to write in a way which will cause your article to become dated quickly, draw out the relevance of your writing to ongoing trends and any important new developments in your field.

4   **Make it look new and important.** Something which obviously seems to be a new treatment of a subject, or a novel approach to an old problem, is more likely to appeal to publishers and editors. A unique contribution is always of more interest than a piece which goes back over well-trodden territory. An article which can be seen as a clear advancement of knowledge or understanding in a field is more likely to be looked on favourably.

5   **Make it appear thorough.** It is important that your writing is taken as credible, even if you're not yet an established writer in the field. Check that your work refers to well-known and respected authorities in the field, and that such references appear quite early.

6   **Make your illustrations good.** Where you use tables, diagrams, charts, and other visual illustrations, make sure that they look good, and that they are well-checked, accurate, and relevant.

7   **Be up-front about seminal research.** If your article reflects something that could be followed up readily by others working in the field, make it clear that there are still many issues to be explored. In such cases include in your writing the unanswered questions and the challenges, rather than trying to make your work look finished and rounded.

8   **Make any controversy overt.** If your article is arguing against accepted views on a topic, let this be seen to be the case from the outset, rather than saving the controversy for your conclusions. Editors will want to be able to decide whether the controversy is a strong reason for publishing your work.

9   **Follow the author guidelines to the letter.** If you're asked to supply three copies, double-spaced and with a wide right-hand margin, do so. When most of the submissions that editors consider are correctly 'in-format', any that are not stand out at once.

10   **Make it readable.** Clarity is probably the most important attribute of tone and style of writing. For your work to be accepted for publication, it is not enough that the editor or referee can understand what you're saying. They probably can understand it, as they're likely to be well versed in the field, but they are working on behalf of readers who may not know the field backwards.

11   **Make it relevant.** Writing that goes off on tangents (however interesting) appeals less to most editors than writing which sticks closely to the agenda spelled out by the title and abstract at the beginning. Those looking at manuscripts can become irritated quite quickly if they feel they are being led on a wild goose chase.

12   **Make the title self-explanatory and interesting.** A good title should whet the appetite of prospective readers. It should indicate not just what the piece is about, but should also hint at why it will be worth reading. The combination of title and sub-title can be an effective way of invoking interest, and adding that first bit of rationale.

13   **Get the abstract perfect.** When your work is in the final stages of being considered for publication, your abstract will be read much more deeply than anything else. Make sure that your article lives up to the promise of its abstract. It is worth rewriting the abstract as many times as may be needed to make sure that it really does summarize the main thrust of your writing and your findings.

45

Diagrams, drawings and tables

Whether you use visual components such as these will depend on your discipline and on the sort of book or article you are writing. If words alone are all you need, count yourself fortunate to have one less area to worry about, and skip this section! However, if diagrams, charts, tables, drawings, graphs, pictures, or any other visual means of communicating data or ideas are relevant to your writing, it's best to set out to use them well from the outset of your writing. The following suggestions will help you avoid the most frustrating pitfalls.

1   **Think about the value of making your writing visual, and not just textual.** For readers, a double-page spread of unbroken text tends to be less attractive than something which is broken up by headings, subheadings, and (above all) *figures*. Not numbers of course, but graphs, diagrams, pictures, tables, charts, flowcharts, sketches – even cartoons. Adding this kind of visual variety to your work can keep your readers engaged.

2   **Read your publisher's guidelines carefully.** Most publishers offer detailed suggestions to authors regarding how best to incorporate visual material into their writing.

3   **Make the quality of your figures suitable for reproduction by your publisher.** The perceived quality of a book is often linked to the clarity and relevance of its illustrations. Many publishers prefer to have masters of figures supplied separately from the text, and in a format which they can reduce (such as an A4 diagram to be reduced to A5, or further, in the actual book). Most publishers insist on original photographs, printouts or drawings, rather than photocopies.

4   **Don't number your figures from 1 to 97.** It is best to code your numbering by chapter. It is easier to alter the number of the figures from Fig 3.4 onwards, when you decide to insert a *new* Fig 3.4 into Chapter 3, than to have to go right through all the following chapters as well.

5   **Check that your figures are correctly referred to in your text.** This is particularly important when you've inserted a new one or deleted one, changing the numbers. It's one of the hardest things for an author to spot, as we all tend to read what we meant to say, rather than what we actually said, and it's even worse with numbers than with words!

6   **Take particular care with figures you may be using from other people's work.** It is not just a matter of acknowledging them, and seeking and getting permission to use them (and probably paying for this). It may well be necessary for you to re-draw a figure to bring it up to the standard that your publisher needs from you to be able to produce it from your manuscript.

7   **Make your captions full and self-explanatory.** It should be possible for readers to get a fairly full impression of what any figure is about even before looking in the text for what you actually say about it.

8   **Try to ensure that your figures will be visible when readers are reading about them.** Few things are more irritating to readers than to have to flip backwards or forwards to look at a figure while reading your description or discussion of it. Publishers usually ask authors to indicate approximately where in the text a figure should appear, such as by inserting:

Figure 3.2 about here

---

9   **Decide whether you need to include a list of figures.** If your illustrations are particularly important, readers may find it useful to be able to return to a specific figure easily, and such a list helps them to do so.

10   **Triple check your figures at proof stage.** Some of the most common errors in proofs relate to the wrong caption being placed with a figure, figures themselves being transposed, figures occasionally being missed out altogether, and figures being wrongly referenced in the text. Then there are all the possibilities of there being something wrong with the figures themselves. It is worth doing a completely separate check through all of your figures, captions and numbers at proof stage. Once you find one mistake, look even more carefully for others. All this is worth the trouble, compared to the possibility of incorrect figures being on your public record.

46

Making a good finish

Making a good last impression is almost as crucial as making a good first one. This applies not only to many of your readers, but also to most reviewers, who tend to take a close look at how you conclude your writing. This is not least so that they can find out what your main conclusions are, and whether they really want to find out all about it by going through your work in detail. The following suggestions may help you reach your conclusions in a robust way.

1   **Decide quite early on what your main conclusions are going to be.** This is best done at the planning stage of your writing. You may feel that you have a wide range of things that are important enough to qualify as main conclusions, but any book, paper or article has its last 100 words.

2   **Work out what you wish your conclusions to achieve.** There are many possibilities, including summarizing a case you have made, or pointing your readers further to possible future developments in the field, or summing up the questions which further research may follow up.

3   **Decide which one impression you would like your readers to go away with.** Ask yourself 'If there's only one thing they will remember, what do I want it to be?' This is likely to be the most suitable basis for your final words.

4   **Take particular care with the wording of your conclusions.** These are the parts of your work which may be most likely to be quoted by others, and you need to protect yourself from the position of having to live with words which you would prefer to have been different.

5   **Keep your conclusions quite short.** Whether you plan your ending as a final climax, or a twist in the tail, or a drawing together of related elements, don't take too long over it, or too many readers may miss the significance you are trying to communicate.

6   **Don't just conclude your piece as a whole.** With books, it is worth reaching a robust concluding section at the end of every chapter, and even in an academic paper or article it's often worth making summaries at the end of each major section.

7   **Don't repeat yourself too obviously.** Readers normally don't like to feel that they are reading something that they have already read. It is possible to reiterate main points in ways that are different. For example, the gist of several conclusions can be gathered together as a bullet-point list.

8   **Don't introduce new material into your conclusions.** The conclusions should be the punch lines that review for your readers where your book has taken them, and summarizes the main arguments as a finale.

9   **Flag your conclusions well.** The heading 'Conclusions' is probably over-used. It does no harm to use a heading which reminds your readers exactly what your conclusions are about. Question headings are useful here, such as 'What causes destabilization? A summary'.

10   **Pilot your conclusions.** Ask as many people as you can to look over your last page or two, and to give you their feedback. Check whether the messages you're trying to deliver are getting across. Ask whether the wording is clear enough. Ask whether it reads interestingly. Also ask particularly for feedback on anything that is not correct, or badly phrased, or ambiguous.

11   **Check that your conclusions are visible in the contents pages.** This helps readers who have not much time to see at least some of the context leading up to your conclusions, and also allows them to locate and read intermediate conclusions or summing up sections in your work.

47

Getting the references right

This can seem boring! It is hard work. Sooner or later, however, you will need to develop your skills to refer to other people's work in the ways that publishers require. A poorly referenced piece of work has every chance of being rejected altogether by a publisher. The suggestions below should help you to do so before you're told to put your references right by your publisher!

1   **Check the format that your publisher normally uses for references.** The main two types are books, and papers in journals. Guidance is normally provided in 'Guidelines for Authors', and such guidelines are particularly crucial for chapters in edited collections and for articles in journals. A common format for referencing books is as follows:
    Brown, S and Race, P (1995) *Assess your own Teaching Quality* Kogan Page, London.

2   **Get the punctuation right!** You may think that this is unimportant, but it is important that in books, edited collections, and particularly in journals, *all* authors provide references in an agreed format. Major publishers normally prefer this to be as simple a format as possible, without quotation marks for titles, and without colons, semi-colons or anything other than a comma between author's family names and forenames or initials.

3   **Find out which system is used for including references in the text.** The most common system is the Harvard one, such as 'Jones (1998) suggests that...'. If there is more than one work published in one year by an author, you may need to use 'Jones (1998a) suggests that...'.

4   **Keep all the necessary details of your sources as you write your book.** Whether you use a card indexing system, or create a database on your computer, you will need such details as author(s)' family name, author(s)' initials or forenames, the exact title of your source, the date of publication, the publisher's name and location(s). For edited collections, you will also need details of the editor(s), and the title of the collection. For journal articles, you will need the volume number and page numbers of the articles.

5   **Remember that your list of references may be the first part of your book or article that referees or reviewers look at.** The quality with which you refer to the available relevant literature is often taken as a measure of the quality of your own work. A good bibliography shows that your work is up to date, and well-researched.

6   **Don't miss out references to important work that you happen not to like.** Some authors seem to wish to pretend that other views on their pet subjects don't exist. It is better to be seen to be taking such work into account (even critically) than to ignore it.

7   **Hesitate to cite anything that is not generally available.** However crucial or relevant the reference may seem to be, few readers take delight in seeing you refer to 'Jones (1997) *Unpublished Report: Factors to Consider in Quality Assessment'*. Even less liked are 'unpublished correspondence', 'conference handout', or even 'PhD Thesis, University of Poppleton'. It is best if readers of your work, wherever they are in the world, have a reasonable chance of being able to track down your sources should they wish to do so.

8   **Prepare yourself to make accurate quotations.** When you quote verbatim any extract from a source, it is important that it is clearly seen as a quotation and is fully acknowledged. It is preferable to quote exactly which page(s) the material comes from, taking care to mention which edition of the book the material may have been drawn from in your reference.

9   **Check your references really carefully at proof stage.** If you have supplied your work on disk, and if you got your references right in the first place, this should be a straightforward task. If, however, someone else has keyed in your references, there will be far more mistakes here than in any other part of your work, not least because the names of your sources will not be familiar to the typist. Also, it is particularly easy to mis-key numbers, dates, or to miss out volume numbers.

10   **If you fall short on any of the suggestions made above, watch out for your author queries!** Publisher's readers and copy-editors are hot on referencing, and will normally list your deficiencies in this aspect at length. Sooner or later, you'll be required to make a good job of it by any reputable publisher, so you may as well learn to do it all correctly at the outset.

48

Writing a glossary

A good glossary can make all the difference when readers really need a kind of dictionary to the acronyms, special language and vocabulary used in the book. The suggestions below should help you to decide whether or not your readers need a glossary from you, and if so, how to go about preparing one.

1   **Decide whether you really need a glossary.** Writing a glossary is quite time consuming, and it is easy to end up with one that would have been better missed out altogether. Don't do one unless there are good reasons for having one.

2   **If you decide to use a glossary, start writing it as soon as you start writing.** It is much more efficient to highlight key words, acronyms and so on as you write your text than to go back at the end looking for them. It also helps you to decide what to spell out as you go in your writing, and when to refer readers to the glossary.

3   **Work out the purposes your glossary will serve.** Some books need glossaries much more than others. For example, if you need to use many acronyms in your book, a glossary can help readers new to the field to make sense of them. Alternatively, if there are many words which have specific meanings in your field, you may wish to include a list of these words with a precise definition showing how the words are to be interpreted in the context of your book.

4   **Think whether it may be better *not* to use acronyms.** While they can make a useful shorthand for readers in your particular field, the extensive use of acronyms can make your book much less attractive to readers from other countries, using other acronyms. If you intend your book to have an international readership, it can be worth thinking of spelling out every acronym on every occasion.

5   **Make lists of acronyms and key words and phrases as you write.** This can save a considerable amount of time going back through your work looking for them at the end, when you decide to make a glossary. Also, keeping these key terms in mind all the way through your writing means that when you come to write definitions of key terms, you have thought about it in advance and are more likely to arrive at well-phrased definitions.

6   **Check your acronyms.** It's worth looking them up in other people's glossaries, just to make sure that you aren't using a local variant of the odd acronym. Also, if you look up dictionaries or reference books containing lists of acronyms, you may be surprised to find that some acronyms have quite different meanings in different discipline areas.

7   **Check your definitions of key words and phrases.** Other books in your field may well have their own lists of terminology, and it is useful to compare your definitions with other people's, and check for consistency, or for intended distinctions.

8   **Bear in mind your intended audience.** Your glossary should be appropriately matched to the levels and experience of your intended readers. If your work is of an advanced nature, you may be wise to avoid including definitions of familiar terms or acronyms, which could come across as condescending or patronizing to your readers. If your work is aimed at beginners, you may want to include many more definitions.

9   **Print out a draft version of your glossary and seek feedback on it.** It can be particularly useful just to get colleagues' reactions to your glossary, especially asking them to comment on whether they agree with your definitions of key words and phrases. Editing in feedback from half a dozen readers can improve a glossary very significantly.

10 **Put page numbers in at proof stage.** It can be very helpful for readers if a glossary also contains references to the page numbers where each term or acronym is introduced in your book. It is also useful to check that your definitions of key terms are in harmony with the way you introduced these terms in the body of your book.

49

Compiling an index

Most books have some kind of index. Book reviews often mention whether or not there is an index, and whether it is a good one. If you're writing your first book you will probably have never yet tried your hand at the task of actually *creating* an index, even though you will have used countless indexes prepared by other people. The suggestions below should not only speed up the task of making an index, but also help you to make a useful one.

1   **Decide whether *you* will do the index.** Publishers are usually willing to sub-contract an index, but it will cost you out of your royalties (typically about £200 or more in the UK). If you're not good at doing an index, it could be money well spent. However, once you have gained the skills to write a good index, you can probably do the best one yourself, as you know your work better than anyone else.

2   **Decide what the index will be for.** It may seem obvious, but there are different kinds of index. In some books, the index is a really important tool to help readers find out exactly where to go to read about particular topics and themes, or about the cited work of selected authors. In other books, the index is just there as a seldom-used appendix (sometimes merely because reviewers tend to grumble if there's no index at all). How much effort and time you put into compiling your index will depend which sort it is intended to be.

3   **Consider whether to have separate author and key word indexes.** If citing other authors' work is a major component of your book, it is probably worth separating the author index from the general one. If less than, say, 50 other authors are mentioned directly, it is usually better just to include their names in a key word index.

4   **Decide whether to have two 'levels' of indexing.** For example, some authors like to put the *main* page references for important key words in bold, with 'the rest' just in plain print. This helps readers to find your main findings or discussion on particular key words. This can be

particularly useful where you mention a topic several times quite early in your book, but where your in-depth discussion is several chapters on from the beginning.

5   **Think about double-entry indexing.** Sometimes there will be more than one word for the same important idea or topic. Indexes that direct readers to 'see…' are annoying, and it is better to copy and paste the page numbers relating to one word to the entry relating to a synonym, making sure, of course, that anyone looking up what has been said about the synonym will know what the actual words are on the pages concerned. For example, if the entry was primarily made for 'assessment', the same page numbers may be relevant for 'measuring achievement (assessment)' where the word in brackets reminds readers of the word they are likely to see on the pages concerned when they look them up.

6   **Decide when to do your index.** The most usual time is at proof stage, as only then do you know what the actual page numbers will be. Even if you've made a draft index at manuscript stage, it can take quite a long time to change all the page numbers to those relating to the actual proofs (and it is a very tedious job, and liable to errors). Therefore, you may well wish to let your publisher know that you will make an index of a given number of pages at proof stage.

7   **Map out the main backbone of the index from your contents pages.** Titles and main headings will contain most of the really important key words, so it is worth getting these down first.

8   **Combine the task of filling out the index with that of proof-reading.** Doing both concurrently helps make both tasks go well. For example, after reading a page or two of proofs (carefully, of course, not just reading!) look back at the pages and decide what they're mainly about and enter your key words into the index page by page.

9   **Try highlighting.** While reading the proofs, it can be useful to use a highlighting pen to mark the most important words and phrases. Most of these will turn out to be relevant for inclusion in your index. Don't just highlight new key words; remember to continue to highlight ones that are already in the index, so that you can add the extra page numbers to those already noted.

10 **Use columns while making your index!** If you're typing in your index on a word-processing package that can produce multiple columns, it can be useful to set up your page for say three columns, which helps save you from having to scroll up and down several pages as your index grows, every time you wish to add a new entry.

11   **Change your index back to single column for your publisher.** Unless you particularly want part of your work to appear in a multiple-column format, it is best to send your manuscript and disk in single column format. The use of columns for making an index is just to make it easier to compile. Leave your publisher to decide whether to print it in double columns or not.

12   **Beware of proof changes that will lead to page changes.** If while proof-reading you find you need to make amendments which may add to or reduce the page length of your book, your indexing could be knocked out. It is best at proof stage to keep amendments and corrections to the absolute minimum, and to try to replace anything that needs replacing by an equivalent number of words.

50

Checking proofs

Most authors hate proof checking. It is much more fun to be creative than to do the tidying-up and housekeeping. However, think ahead to the day of publication. Imagine reading your work, full of pride and satisfaction, then getting that sinking feeling as you see in print errors, missed words, unfinished sentences, wrong captions on diagrams, and such like. These will now be on public record at least until your next edition! The following suggestions may help you to prevent such nightmares becoming a reality for you.

1   **Find out when your proofs are expected to be ready.** It is worth liaising with your editor in the weeks leading up to this stage, so that you can make available enough time to check them thoroughly. Turn round times for proofs are frequently measured in days, or two weeks at best.

2   **Set aside some time to check your proofs.** Once you know when your proofs will be delivered, confirm with your editor that you will have a specific time window when you will give them your attention.

3   **Make sure you know how, when and where your proofs will be delivered.** If they are to be left at your work address, make sure that the people who handle incoming mail are expecting them. We know of some proofs that were sent by air mail right around the world, only to be returned with 'not known at this address' from the institution where the author was waiting for them!

4   **Read your publisher's instructions carefully.** Check exactly how you are to mark up your proofs. Normally there are strict guidelines, such as 'correct errors in red', 'indicate corrections in the margin as well as in the text', or 'make minor changes and additions that are not corrections in blue' (and remember you may have to pay for these out of your royalties). Some publishers will send you a sheet of terminology and codes to use in marking up proofs; these can be somewhat daunting at first sight, but in practice you will probably only need to use a small cross-section of the mark up language.

5   **Don't just read your proofs!** The biggest danger with reading what you've written is that you see what you *meant*, and don't always see what is actually printed there. Reading proofs is an activity that has to be done much more slowly and deliberately than normal reading. It can be worth getting someone to read out aloud your manuscript version, and check up that everything is there. Having said this, expect to find all sorts of minor adjustments to your language and style, which may have been done by your publisher's copy-editors. With such adjustments, always check that the points you were intending to make are still coming through.

6   **Resist the temptation of second thoughts.** When it is really important to make changes other than corrections at proof stage, it can still be done. However, it can be an expensive business, especially if it may alter the page numbers (and therefore the index, glossary, contents list, and so on). Only make changes if they are absolutely necessary, such as when a major development has happened since the book was written, and needs to be mentioned in the body of the text rather than in a 'postscript' added on at the end of the book.

7   **Take particular care with corrections that could affect subsequent pagination.** If, for example, a paragraph has been missed out accidentally, inserting it could alter all the pages that follow, and have knock-on effects on the index, contents pages, and so on. In such circumstances, it may be advisable to try to make the correction without affecting the page structure. This could mean editing down some other parts of the page concerned.

8   **Check danger areas particularly well.** The places where errors are most likely include parts that may have not have been transcribed directly from your manuscript (or disk), such as contents pages, alterations that you made on the basis of Author Queries, and any other changes made since the first submission of your manuscript. Double-check photographs, figures and captions. Are they in the right place? Does the caption match the figure? Are the figures correctly referenced in the text? It is all too easy just to read through the proofs without ever noticing serious errors that can happen in these areas.

9   **Watch out for 'Friday afternoon sections'!** When you find two or more mistakes close together, it could be that the copy-editor or typesetter was having an off moment, so look even harder for other mistakes. They tend to come in clusters.

10   **Meet or exceed the publisher's deadline.** It is probable that the publication window for your book will be critically dependent on the proofs being received by the due date. If your book misses this window, it could be some time before it will be processed.

11   **Make copies of pages containing important alterations.** It is not often that a set of marked-up proofs goes missing in the post, but we know of occasions when it has happened. It takes far longer to do all the alterations again than to make some copies. Also, it is an indescribably frustrating experience going again through proofs trying to remember where the corrections and adjustments were needed.

12   **Parcel the marked-up proofs securely.** Address the package clearly, for example, 'For the attention of Ms Jones at ...'. Also mark the package 'Marked up proofs'; publishers know how important these particular packages are.

13   **Check that your proofs have actually been received.** It's worth telling your editor that you have sent them off, and which delivery service you have used. Telephoning to confirm that they have arrived is well worth the trouble for the peace of mind that it brings.

51

Copyright and rights

The Concise Oxford English Dictionary of Current Usage (Oxford University Press, 1996, Ninth edition) defines the noun 'copyright' as 'the exclusive legal rights given to the originator or his or her assignee for a fixed number of years, to print, publish, perform, film or record literary, artistic or musical material, and to authorize others to do the same'. Confusion and misunderstandings on points related to copyright are common among authors. If you do run into substantial problems, you will need to contact a legal copyright specialist, but the following tips should help you to firm up your own understanding of these issues and, we hope, help you to avoid major problems.

1   **Be clear about what the term copyright actually means.** As defined above, if you are the author of an original piece of work, you are the copyright holder. By signing a contract, you are usually making the publisher your assignee or appointed representative.

2   **Understand what is meant by the term 'rights'.** As a copyright owner, rights are what you may legally or morally claim for your work, which are all collectively protected by the term of copyright.

3   **Be clear which rights you are assigning to your publisher when you sign the contract.** All the possible subsidiary publishing-related rights are generally covered in a publisher's standard contract. Make sure that your contract sets out what you want and what you have agreed with your publisher. Remember that you may make exceptions to the rights you assign to your publisher, for example, retaining electronic rights, if you do so at the contract stage.

4   **Refer to the appropriate law.** In the UK at the time of writing, issues relating to British copyright are covered by the Copyright Acts of 1956 and 1988. Copies of the document containing the 1988 Act in full can be obtained from The Stationery Office (formerly HMSO).

5   **Remember that copyright law operates internationally.** Most countries have their own laws. Your work will be protected internationally under the copyright law of the country in which your work is originally published.

6   **Consult an expert if you have a copyright query or a legal difficulty.** Copyright law is a complex area. If someone contacts you complaining that you have breached his or her copyright, or makes a rights-related request to you, take advice before replying. Refer all queries to your publisher initially. If a problem persists, you will need to consult a specialist lawyer.

7   **Note that copyright exists for the period of the originator's lifetime and for seventy years after the originator's death.** If the work becomes a great commercial success, the copyright will become a valuable commodity. This means that, as an author, you are entitled to receive royalty payments for all forms licensed during your lifetime.

8   **Look to the future!** You will need to make your wishes known about who you would like to manage your copyright property after your death, how, and who will benefit financially from any earned revenue.

9   **If your work goes out of print and your publisher does not plan to reprint it, rights and copyright usually revert to you.** Remember that any rights, including copyright control, are assigned to your publisher under the terms of your contract and the contract remains valid so long as the publisher is making your work available. Subsidiary rights licensed under the contract usually remain valid until after rights have reverted.

10 **Clarify the reverting rights.** Most contracts include a clause about reversion of rights when a book goes out of print and it is worthwhile to ask your publisher to officially clarify this in writing if this happens. You are then free to approach other publishers if the topic regains popularity, in either revised or unrevised formats. You are then also free to license rights on your work in another format.

11 **Be very wary of ever signing away your copyright in a work.** Never be so keen to get your work published that you sign an agreement that hands over the actual copyright to the publisher for a fee. While few book publishers will request this, it is still quite common practice with journal articles, commissioned work and in the music industry. If you do sign away your copyright, your publisher will be able to make all future decisions regarding your work's publication without consulting you. A big fee may sound attractive initially, but if your work really did take off, you could stand to lose a lot.

12   **Take great care not to infringe other people's copyright.** Most authors and their publishers do not usually object to the use of copyright material so long as it is properly acknowledged. However, it is sensible to seek permission when you plan to quote lengthy extracts or to use any figures or illustrations from a published work.

13   **Be clear about what you can do.** For example, the Copyright Acts of 1956 and 1988 in the UK advise that permissions be sought for the reproduction of copyright prose work for an extract longer than 400 words, a series of extracts totalling more than 800 words, where one extract is longer than 300 words and an extract or series of extracts comprising a quarter or more of a work. Permission should *always* be sought when wishing to reproduce poetry, song lyrics, reported speech and all illustrations and diagrams.

14   **Allow plenty of time to seek copyright clearance.** This often takes longer than expected, so you need to allow plenty of time for correspondence well before you submit the manuscript, in case permission is refused and you need to rewrite, or if permissions are a long time in coming.

52

What *is* publication?

In most contexts, writers are quite clear about what constitutes publication. However, if your work is in any way meant to be secret or confidential, the boundaries can become blurred. Furthermore, if you are in the process of having something new you have discovered patented, you will need to be even more careful about the precise meaning of publication. We hope the following notes will help you gain a feel for the different kinds of publication that exist.

1   **What is the legal definition of 'publication'?** Something counts as having been published if it forms 'part of the state of the art' in the discipline involved. In European patent law, this is defined as 'everything made available to the public by means of a written or oral description, by use, or in any other way'. This, at its most extreme, means to any one member of the public, anywhere in the world.

2   **How can you keep something confidential?** In legal terms, something can only be deemed to be confidential if any persons to whom it is to be disclosed have indicated their agreement to keep it confidential through a written 'Confidentiality Agreement'. This means that in any of the normal processes which you are likely to follow in your bid to get your work published, you are likely to be in the position of having given up any strong legal claim to confidentiality. The exact date from which your work is regarded as having been published varies, however, and some indications of how this varies through different publication channels are given below.

3   **Scholarly papers in journals, and articles in magazines and newspapers.** Legally, these are counted as being published from the first day that an ordinary reader could get hold of a copy of the paper. This is not the same date as the journals arrived at the distribution warehouse from the printers. The publication date is defined as the first date that the article is available to the public, and not just to subscribers to the journal or magazine.

4   **Abstracts.** If you write an abstract for a conference presentation and allow the abstract to be distributed in advance to delegates, or to be available at the conference reception desk, either of these constitutes publication of your abstract. If there is anything in your abstract that is under consideration for patenting, the patent application needs to be filed before such publication.

5   **Theses.** Sometimes oral examinations are held in public, and in such cases the thesis is counted as published by the examination itself. Usually, however, publication starts from the date when a reader could first get hold of the thesis from a shelf in the university library (and not when the first reader actually *does* take the volume from the shelf). This date may be different from the cataloguing or accession date in the library.

6   **Messages on the Internet and e-mail communications.** These count as published from the day of posting. This means that if your message can be read east of the international date line, your message is actually published on the day before you sent it. Removing a message from the Internet does not cancel the fact that it has been published, as the message could continue to exist anywhere that it has been downloaded or copied.

7   **Messages to restricted audiences.** Electronic messages to newsgroups or bulletin boards count as having been published as soon as they are available to any member of the group, even if they are intended to be confidential to the group. The 'confidential disclosure to many people' situation counts as publication, if the information is available to a significant cross-section of the people who are active in the field concerned.

8   **Poster displays.** These count as a publication if they are mounted in a place such as a corridor where members of the public can actually see them.

9   **Exhibitions and open days.** Materials on show at exhibitions or open events are deemed to be published, to the extent that a specialist looking at the material exhibited could understand what was on show.

10 **Oral or casual disclosures.** At a conference, if you depart from your prepared text to answer a question for example, that answer is considered to be published. The same applies to remarks made informally, unless everyone present knows and accepts that your remarks are intended to be kept secret.

(These guidelines about the meaning of 'publication' are adapted from *Publish and Be Damned: how to avoid inadvertent publication of your invention* by BMG plc, London.)

Chapter 6   Electronic publishing

53   New models of publishing
54   Advantages and disadvantages of electronic publishing
55   Publishing in e-journals
56   Using electronic means to support traditional publishing

Our final chapter is quite short, but in some ways it addresses an area that is growing in importance even more rapidly than all the other forms of publication mentioned in earlier chapters: 'electronic publishing'. In a book of this size, we can only hope to alert you to the pace of change in this area, and hopefully to whet your appetite to try your hand both at using electronic journals for appropriate purposes relating to your own writing or research, and also to make good use of electronic communication, information searching and retrieval to support your research.

New models of publishing that may eventually supersede traditional publishing form the basis of the next set of tips that we provide. These are followed by a set explaining what are the advantages and disadvantages of using electronic publishing at this current time, taking into account the trends in academic publishing.

Traditional journals are often supplemented or replaced by journals in electronic form, and we next supply some thoughts on how to maximize the potential of e-journals.

Finally in this chapter we explore ways of using electronic means to support traditional publishing in the transitional period before, perhaps, they overtake papyrocentric publication altogether.

53

New models of publishing

Electronic publishing, or e-publishing, is not just replicating the forms of traditional publishing – it is creating new ones too. Here we offer some tips on why and how you might expand from traditional models of publishing into something virtually different.

1   **Review your objectives.** E-publishing isn't for everyone. As we explore in a later section, there are distinct advantages and disadvantages involved. Make sure you know why the electronic medium interests you. You will be targeting this channel just as you would any other publisher, so make sure it's right for you.

2   **Create your own homepage.** Many Internet providers offer advice and good financial deals to help you set up your own site. This will help people to find you by entering the appropriate key words when they access a search engine.

3   **Create virtual communities.** Your interest area can be represented by a conference, a site, a journal, a discussion group, a list of e-mail addresses – the possibilities are only confined by your imagination.

4   **Invent ways to collaborate (e-mail forum groups).** You can join a discussion group in your interest area, or even start your own. All you need is an e-mail address, and the e-mails of some people you would like to share ideas with. Follow the instructions on your e-mail software to set up a discussion group to share ideas.

5   **Invent new ways to review papers.** You can post papers for general discussion and feedback from whomever, or you can offer papers for general reading but feedback from only a select few, or you can offer papers electronically to only your reviewers – or a combination of these and other methods. The draw of virtual publishing is often the wider access and dissemination it allows.

6   **Review your deadlines.** Potential collaborators and reviewers are usually busy people, so the fact that we are now operating electronically is only one factor which may influence the speed of response. Electronics impact mostly on our ability to capture multi-source feedback almost simultaneously.

7   **Update your material.** Consider your material a live source of knowledge. If you publish a paper on the Internet, work with the publisher to agree an updating schedule. This means you can periodically add to your paper as your research continues. Otherwise, you might as well put it on a shelf in the library.

8   **Become a publisher.** Through your own site you can attract potential authors and create your own e-journal. The cost of promoting and publishing on the Internet is much less than traditional methods. You will still have to establish a reputation.

9   **Validate your work by other sources.** The Internet is comparatively young, and therefore people are still enthusiastic and willing to learn about the medium. Consider linking your own new site to other more mature sites with established reputations.

10 **Use electronic publishing as a way to build your networks.** It can give you a rapid way of getting to know at least some of the people working in your field. You can then use these contacts you make to help you publish in traditional ways as well as electronically.

54

Advantages and disadvantages of electronic publishing

Debate continues over the best medium for publishing today. Ardent protectors of traditional publishing argue that it is the only way to protect the established academic community and its standards; proponents of electronic publishing believe those are exactly the right reasons to move to newer, more experimental methods. Neither are right or wrong; the most innovative approaches combine both. We can summarize here key points of the issue, which may help you decide what works best for you.

1   **Traditional publishing has established processes.** Little is being invented in the traditional paper-based publishing field. That means authors can learn easily how to work the system. Electronic publishing processes, however, are being created as we write, making it less obvious to new authors what approach to use and how.

2   **Electronic publishing has newer, more fluid processes.** The medium is being invented and changed all the time. That means authors can become pioneers in a new channel of communication and influence its development.

3   **Review methods are firmly established in traditional publishing.** People who review journals are well-known, respected members of their fields. The review method – at the very least, double-blind – is well tested and tried. Authors can be confident that their papers will be subjected to rigorous and widely accepted methods of review.

4   **Electronic publishing offers a mix of review methods.** A criticism of the traditional review method is the 'old boy network' nature of the established academic community. People attracted to electronic possibilities tend to be younger and more open to new ideas. This may appeal to an author whose work challenges existing paradigms.

5   **Traditional publishing is slow.** It takes anywhere from a few months to more than a year to get published in a paper-based journal. For people in fast-moving fields this may mean their papers are out of date before they appear in print.

6   **Publishing in e-journals may be quicker.** It depends on the review method, but certainly gathering feedback from a number of different sources can be smoother and faster using e-mail and the Internet.

7   **Traditional publishing offers admission to an elite element of the academic community.** It's hard to become published in the best journals. The older, more established publications have rejection rates that reflect the vast number of people trying to break in. When an author succeeds, the kudos is palatable.

8   **Electronic publishing offers open access to a wider community.** Many e-journals have review methods as stringent as their paper-based counterparts, but discussion groups and other forms of electronic conferencing are accessible to almost anyone.

9   **Not everyone yet has easy access to electronic journals.** For example, some academics who may be leaders in your field may not have got into electronic communication. Some may have only limited or shared access to computer terminals. In some countries, access to information technology may be much more limited than you might expect. The electronic audience, therefore, may not be fully representative of your subject audience.

10   **The audience still counts.** Whatever your ambition as an author, if you remember that your purpose is to communicate with a selected group of people, then the method of communicating becomes simply a matter of which channel works best when. Many authors today use multiple channels, moving easily between trade journals, e-journals, newspapers, scholarly journals, television, radio and other media.

55

Publishing in e-journals

Many thousands of e-journals exist on every imaginable subject. Some are published by individuals, while others are backed by commercial or institutional publishers. Many are only available on the Internet, while others are electronic versions of paper-based publications. Sometimes you are published electronically by default – sometimes you have a choice. Here are some tips about how to do it, whether you want to or not.

1 **Whose work is it, anyway?** Being published electronically may not be what you have in mind, but it may happen anyway. When you publish in a paper-based publication, check the contract. Many publishers assume the rights for electronic publication when they publish on paper.

2 **Should you object to being published electronically?** Authors who resist the kind of blanket copyright clauses described above usually do so on principle. The intellectual ownership of one's work is already established, but the choice to distribute it in any particular way is initially the author's. There are many advantages to electronic publishing, and you may not feel in a position to argue anyway. It is, however, important that you check it out and reach your own conclusion.

3 **Target your journals.** Just as we discussed in Chapter 4, authors must select the journal appropriate to the subject and audience. There will be as many or more choices available electronically as on paper.

4 **But is it respectable?** Some members of the academic community resist electronic publishing because they think it is without standards, reputation and form. They're right, of course, and they're wrong. Respectability varies according to the journal and how its business is conducted, not the medium.

5   **Establish its standards.** There's no reason in theory that an e-journal should be any less rigorous than a paper-based journal. The problem really lies with those who support it. You can find out who reviews and editorially guides the journal by accessing its site.

6   **Read it regularly.** Just as with a paper-based journal, e-journals exist to fulfil a need and meet an editorial objective. Log onto the site and read not only the notes to contributors, but also the articles.

7   **Offer comment.** Many e-journals have different levels of review – one for open access and another for a selected review board. Take the opportunity to offer comment when you're capable of doing so. The feedback you give may generate useful discussion which will impact on your potential paper.

8   **Adhere to submission guidelines.** Like any journal, e-journals have specific housestyle and other requirements which need to be met. Before submitting a paper, ensure you download and understand all the submission requirements.

9   **Encourage updating.** A unique feature of electronic publishing is the possibility of continuous improvement. E-journals should be encouraged to offer mechanisms for regular updates by authors and incorporation of readers' comments.

10 **Understand copyright issues.** Depending on the journal, your work may be available for certain periods of time, to certain other sites, to readers to download and even for conversion to paper-based text. You may or may not object to any of these, but avoid future misunderstandings by agreeing it all at the outset.

56

Using electronic means to support traditional publishing

The Internet has brought profound changes to the publishing industry. In this section we look at some of the ways electronics can help you get published, how you can use the Internet to find information on people and ideas, and what electronics mean to you as an author.

1   **Search for collaborators.** The world is getting smaller and more accessible daily as more people and organizations get e-mail addresses and Internet sites. If you are interested in finding one or more collaborators, try running a search on topic areas you are interested in and follow the links.

2   **Join a discussion group.** Many interest areas sponsor discussion groups and welcome new members. All you need to do is to follow their joining instructions and watch how the dialogue unfolds. Soon, you'll feel confident enough to contribute.

3   **Be specific in your searches.** The Internet has several million sites, and a search for a very common keyword like 'quality' will bring up many thousands of references. Look to narrow your search to find what you need! If you are researching tourism in Iran, ask your search engine for 'tourism in Iran' rather than just 'tourism'.

4   **Search for references.** Do you remember the name or author of a book, but don't have a record of the publication details? Try online bookshops such as amazon.com which have comprehensive search engines for books both in and out of print.

5   **See who else is publishing in your field.** However obscure your area of interest, it is likely that there will be, somewhere in the world, an electronic journal (e-journal) related to it, and a discussion forum (newsgroup) where people share ideas. Use the Deja News search engine to search news-groups.

6   **E-mail potential collaborators.** Don't be shy! One of the greatest values of the Internet and e-mail is the way it opens access worldwide to people and institutions. If you see someone's e-mail address and you're interested in exchanging views or ideas, just drop a line.

7   **Ask for help.** Try sending a proposal or the outline of a paper to a select group of individuals. Even people you've never met may be willing to look at your work and respond.

8   **Use electronic means to help you to get a worldwide view.** You may be surprised to find out about work going on in countries that you just had no idea about as being part of the research community in your subject. Getting feedback from colleagues internationally can help you to get a wider perspective, and may well point you to new directions you can take in your own research.

9   **Consider using electronic communication to help you to undertake research.** When you are able to use electronic means to target appropriate constituencies, such as by asking people to fill in questionnaires electronically, or to respond to open questions, you may be able to gain lots of useful data for your research.

10 **The medium doesn't change the message.** Just because we do things electronically doesn't mean we do them totally differently. Don't expect everyone to volunteer to speak openly on an electronic conference when they wouldn't in a live setting. Be patient.

Conclusions

We hope that you have enjoyed (or are continuing to enjoy) using this book, and that you find the advice provided here useful. The nature of publishing means that not everyone who submits writing for publication will be successful, nor will every successful writer achieve 100 per cent publication of their output. How will you know whether you have been successful in getting yourself published? We list below some performance indicators, not in order of merit, that we as authors use to judge ourselves on our own achievements.

We feel that we have been successful if our:

- writing appears in print in a context of which we feel proud;
- · published outputs are counted towards research output assessment indicators in our field;
- work is reviewed in publications we regard as relevant and reputable, and all the better if the reviews are favourable;
- published work is useful to us in our own professional lives, such as finding uses as aids to teaching;
- readers contact us to ask us questions, make comments, or offer suggestions for future publications or next editions;
- work leads to invitations to us to visit other places and talk further about it.

Although we now get involved in quite a wide variety of different kinds of writing, we still well remember those crucial first steps we took on the journey to publication. We remember the puzzlement at all of those clauses in the first contracts we were given! We remember the pride of seeing our names on our first publications, and seeing our first-ever copies on a bookshop shelf. We remember too seeing the first spelling mistake or misplaced diagram caption in our work! We remember both the glow that we experienced from the first positive review, and the deep gloom from the first critical one! We remember the midnight oil spent before more than one nearly missed deadline. Getting published is, however, quite addictive, and we don't feel ready to stop just yet!

Good luck in getting your own work published, whatever your subject, and in whatever the format you've selected. See you in print!

Dolores Black
Sally Brown
Abby Day
Phil Race

And the last word...

Let's not forget that writing, like genius, can be described as 90 per cent perspiration and 10 per cent inspiration. Hard work, yes, but fun and fulfilling. And so we conclude by offering you, in no particular order, some thoughts expressed by other writers...

1   If you told me to write a love song tonight, I'd have a lot of trouble. But if you tell me to write a love song about a girl with a red dress who goes into a bar and is on her fifth Martini and is falling off her chair, that's a lot easier, and it makes me free to say anything I want. (Stephen Sondheim)

2   The art of writing is the art of applying the seat of the pants to the seat of the chair. (Mary Heaton Vorse)

3   What I adore is supreme professionalism. I'm bored by writers who can write only when it is raining. (Noel Coward)

4   There are very few writers who are not cranks in some way. (Paul Theroux)

5   Always grab the reader by the throat in the first paragraph, sink your thumbs into his windpipe in the second, and hold him against the wall until the tag line. (Paul O'Neil)

6   You can't wait for inspiration. You have to go after it with a club. (Jack London)

7   Any work of art, provided it springs from a sincere motivation to further understanding between people, is an act of faith and therefore is an act of love. (Truman Capote)

8   You always feel when you look it in the eye that you could have put more into it, could have let yourself go and dug harder. (Emily Carr)

9   What I had to face, the very bitter lesson that everyone who wants to write has got to learn, was that a thing may in itself be the finest piece of writing one has ever done, and yet have absolutely no place in the manuscript one hopes to publish. (Thomas Wolfe)

10   The only time I know that something is true is at the moment I discover it in the act of writing. (Jean Malaquais)

11   I write as straight as I can, just as I walk as straight as I can, because that is the best way to get there. (H G Wells)

12   If you write a hundred short stories and they're all bad, that doesn't mean you've failed. You fail only when you stop writing. (Ray Bradbury)

13   If you can change your style, why stick to one style? Style is a vanity because it gives you product identification. (Norman Mailer)

14   Not everything has a name. Some things lead us into a realm beyond words... By means of art we are sometimes sent – dimly, briefly – revelations unattainable by reason. (Aleksandr Solzhenitsyn)

Further reading

Brande, D (1983) *On Becoming a Writer* Macmillan, London.

Bryson, B (1984) *The Penguin Dictionary of Troublesome Words* Penguin, Harmondsworth.

Curran, S (1990) *How to write a book and get it published* Thorsons, Wellingborough.

Day, A (1996) *How to get your research published in journals* Gower, Aldershot.

Derricourt, R (1996) *Ideas into books* Penguin (Australia) and Princeton University Press, Princeton, NJ.

Norman, S (ed.) (1996) *Copyright in further and higher education (3rd Edition)* Library Association Publishing, London.

Partridge, E (1994) *Usage and Abusage* Hamish Hamilton, London.

Sadler, D R (1990) *Up the publication road* HERDSA Publications, Australia.

Strunk, W and White, E B (1979) *The Elements of Style* Macmillan, New York.

Woolcott, L A and Unwin, W R (1983) *Mastering Business Communication*, Macmillan, London.

Index

abstracts   40, 113, 132
acknowledgements   16, 106, 111
advisors   49
agents   2
assessment indicators   143
audiences   6, 61, 67, 70, 75, 87, 93, 96,
    107, 112, 121, 132, 137
author guidelines (*see* notes for authors)
author queries   73, 74, 119, 126

book proposals   51, 60–67
    contents   51–2, 63
    modifying   55
    multiple submissions of   54, 64
    researching for   69
    submitting   51–2, 54, 64, 77
    timescales   51–2, 65–6, 70
    writing   51–2, 63–4
book-signing events   75, 82
brainstorming ideas   12, 24, 56–71
bulletin boards   132

call for papers   40
camera ready copy (or artwork)   62, 78
checklist   44, 49, 60
citation index   15, 59
citation search   86
clearing copyright permissions   36
clipping services   59
co-authoring   11, 31–5, 51, 77, 81, 99
communication systems   34, 49–50, 136
competition   61, 69–70
conclusion   116–17
conferences   7, 71, 75, 132, 134
conference proceedings   2, 7, 29, 40–41
contents list   60
contracts   51–2, 63, 65, 66, 77–9, 82–3,
    138, 143
co-publishing   68
copyright   16, 78, 103–4, 128–30, 138,
    139

deadlines   35, 45, 66, 97, 126, 135, 143
delivery date   62, 77

design   74
diagrams (*see* also figures and tables)
    41, 78, 83, 103, 113, 114–15, 125, 130,
    143
discount   83
display copies (books)   72
draft manuscripts   103, 106
    editing   34, 39

e-(electronic) journals   133, 135, 137,
    138–9
e-mail   34, 45, 49, 75, 111, 132, 134, 137,
    140–41
edited volumes   2, 29, 44–6
editorial objectives (journals)   47–8, 87,
    139
electronic conferencing   137
electronic formats   2, 78
electronic publishing   133–42
establishing a market (books)   51, 69–70

feedback   121, 134
    getting   14, 21, 36, 49, 64, 66, 96, 100,
        110
    giving   31, 139
    responding to   84–5, 98–9, 137, 141
figures (*see* also diagrams and tables)
    78, 115, 126, 130
flyers (promotional)   71–2, 76
foreword   103, 105–6
footnotes   33

glossary   103–4, 120–21, 126

hit-rates   84, 96–7
home market   67
home page   134
house style   48, 97

illustrations (*see* diagrams, figures and
    tables)
index   31, 36, 46, 78, 103–4
    compiling an index   118, 122–4, 126
    author   122

keyword   122
information sources   58–9
intellectual property   40
international
    markets   67
    readers   67, 120
    sales   61, 67–8
internet   132, 135, 137, 138, 140–41
interviews   75
introduction   18, 68, 103, 105–6

jargon   67, 93, 107

key points   41, 47–8
key selling points   63
key words   13, 56, 58, 120–21, 122–3,
    134, 140

launches   2, 34, 51, 52, 75–6
length
    manuscripts   61–2, 77
    sentences   28, 93, 101, 107
literature searches   84, 90–91

mailing lists   75
mapping ideas   56–7
marketing (books)   51, 71–2, 73, 75
mind-mapping   24
model chapters   44
money matters   51, 52, 80–83
monographs   29, 80

net receipts (royalties)   80–81
news agencies   59
news groups   132, 140
notes for authors/editors   60, 87, 109,
    112, 118

objective setting   40
on-line databases   69
on-line searches   15, 59
originator   128–9
outline (journal proposal)   20, 26, 141
overview   18, 35, 51, 56–7

patenting   131–2
peer recognition   6, 35
permissions (and fees)   78, 83, 115, 130
planning techniques   35

popular publishing   2, 29, 37–9
preface   103, 105–6
press releases   38, 76
print runs   80
production schedules   74
project management   34
promotion   73, 74, 80
promotional materials (*see* also flyers)
    106
proofs   31, 36, 73–4, 103–4, 106, 115, 119,
    121, 123, 125–7
publication dates   51–2, 75, 81, 106, 125,
    129, 131
publicity   75
publisher's guidelines   63
punctuation   95, 107–8, 112, 118
purpose   18, 27, 48–9, 88, 105

quality control systems   45

referees   84, 98, 101, 113, 119
references   16, 33, 36, 74, 87, 90, 91, 103,
    109, 112, 119, 140
referencing systems   33, 118,
    Harvard   118
rejection   7, 38, 84–5, 86, 89, 97, 100–102,
    137
reprint   129
research productivity evaluations   9, 32
retaining focus   48
review copies   76
review process   21, 22, 86
reviewers   30, 49, 50, 69, 73, 76, 89, 91,
    96–7, 98–9, 101, 111, 112, 116, 119,
    122, 134, 135
rights   78, 79, 103–4, 128–30, 138
royalties   8, 9, 35, 79, 80–3, 125, 129
    escalating royalty rates   80
    royalty advances   79, 81
    royalty rates   80
    royalty statements   79, 82

sample chapters   61
scanning   73
scope (of journal articles)   86, 89, 90–91
secondary sources   59
selecting contributors   44
selecting papers   2, 29, 47–8
source material   4–5, 15–17, 22, 58, 118

spell-check   23, 95
standard terms (contracts)   77
style   28, 29, 38, 44, 84, 87, 92, 95, 112, 146
subsidiary rights   77, 79
synopsis   38, 55, 56, 60, 63

tables   41, 62, 103, 113, 114–15
targeting
   journals   84, 86–7
   a publishing company   51, 53–5
timescales   51, 75, 82, 106
title   60, 74, 113, 123
translation   68

unique selling points   69

virtual communities   134
virtual publishing   134
voice (authorial)   44, 84, 92–3

web-sites   15, 87
word counts   57, 61
word processing formats/packages   10, 45, 62, 73, 92, 109
world rights   78–9
writing collaboratively (*see* also co-authors)   2, 29, 31–5
writer's block   25–6